The Achievement of Michael Oakeshott

Michael Oakeshott as a young man.

The Achievement of Michael Oakeshott

edited by

Jesse Norman

Duckworth

First published in 1993 by
Gerald Duckworth & Co. Ltd.
The Old Piano Factory
48 Hoxton Square, London N1 6PB
Tel: 071 729 5986
Fax: 071 729 0015

Preface and editorial arrangement
© 1993 by A.J. Norman.
Contributions © 1993 by named authors:
J.L. Auspitz, R. Price, K. Minogue, J. Casey, T. Fuller, J. Hart,
E. Kedourie, N. O'Sullivan, J. Liddington.

All rights reserved. No part of this publication
may be reproduced, stored in a retrieval system, or
transmitted, in any form or by any means, electronic,
mechanical, photocopying, recording or otherwise,
without the prior permission of the publisher.

A catalogue record for this book
is available from the British Library

ISBN 0 7156 2451 2

Photoset in North Wales by
Derek Doyle & Associates, Mold, Clwyd.
Printed in Great Britain by
Redwood Press Limited, Melksham.

Contents

	Contributors	vii
	Preface	ix
1.	Michael Joseph Oakeshott (1901-1990) *Josiah Lee Auspitz*	1
2.	A Choice and Master Spirit *Russell Price*	26
3.	Modes and Modesty *Kenneth Minogue*	43
4.	Philosopher of Practice *John Casey*	58
5.	The Poetics of the Civil Life *Timothy Fuller*	67
6.	The Civilised Imperative *Jeffrey Hart*	82
7.	The History of Political Thought Seminar *Kenneth Minogue*	87
8.	A Colleague's View *Elie Kedourie*	97
9.	In the Perspective of Western Thought *Noel O'Sullivan*	101
10.	Bibliography *John Liddington*	107
	Index	145

Contributors

Josiah Lee Auspitz is Secretary of the Sabre Foundation and Director of its philosophical programmes. 'Michael Joseph Oakeshott (1901-90)' appeared under a slightly different title in the Summer 1991 issue of the *American Scholar*.

Russell Price is Senior Lecturer in Politics at Lancaster University. A shorter version of his memoir appeared in the October 1991 issue of the *Cambridge Review*.

Kenneth Minogue is Professor of Political Science at the London School of Economics and Political Science. 'Modes and Modesty' appeared under the title 'A Memoir: Michael Oakeshott (1901-90)' in *Political Studies* (1991), XXXIX. 'The History of Political Thought Seminar' appeared in the October 1991 issue of the *Cambridge Review*.

John Casey is a Fellow of Gonville and Caius College, Cambridge. 'Philosopher of Practice' appeared under the title 'Michael Oakeshott 1901-90' in the November 1991 issue of the *Caian*.

Timothy Fuller is Dean of the College and Professor of Political Science at Colorado College. A shorter version of 'The Poetics of the Civil Life' appeared under the title 'Michael Oakeshott (1901-90)' in the Summer 1991 issue of *Political Theory*.

Jeffrey Hart is Professor of English at Dartmouth College, New Hampshire. 'The Civilised Imperative' is a modified version of an obituary of Oakeshott which appeared in the *National Review* of January 28, 1991.

Contributors

Elie Kedourie was, until his death in 1992, Emeritus Professor of Politics at the London School of Economics and Political Science. 'A Colleague's View' was delivered under the title 'Michael Oakeshott' as an address at Oakeshott's memorial service in May 1991. It is printed here as delivered.

Noel O'Sullivan is Reader in Politics at the University of Hull. 'In the Perspective of Western Thought' appeared as an obituary in the *Independent* on December 22, 1990.

John Liddington, formerly of Balliol College, Oxford, is a solicitor with Speechley Bircham in London.

Preface

The public reaction to the death of Michael Oakeshott in December 1990 was in contrast to the rather slender press which he received during his lifetime. After the obituary hubbub had died down, however, it could be observed that a rather quieter, slower celebration was in progress; a wake, one might say, in which various of Oakeshott's friends, pupils and admirers paid their respects to the deceased, as much to record a personal as to record a philosophical debt. A long memoir appeared in the *American Scholar*; another in the *Times Literary Supplement*; a third, perhaps unexpectedly, in the *New Republic*, and a fourth in Oakeshott's old college annual the *Caian*. So it went on, back and forth across the Atlantic, for almost a year.

After a while, common features began to show through. Almost all the essays were carefully modulated meditations, treating the philosopher and his ideas as a single whole. Few paid any direct attention to contemporary academic debates. In revisiting much the same theoretical ground, they presented differences of emphasis and interest, both with Oakeshott and with one other, in a spirit of generosity and restraint.

Nine of the essays have now been collected into this book. To them has been added a comprehensive new bibliography, the first to have been published since 1976.

It only remains to thank those without whom publication would have been impossible: the contributors, both for their essays and other assistance; John Liddington, for his heroic efforts to catalogue a quickly burgeoning Oakeshott literature; those who improved or amended the resulting bibliography; and the directors and officers of the Sabre Foundation, under whose auspices the book was originally conceived and funded. Specific thanks are also due to Shirley Robin Letwin; Ferdinand Mount; Sylvia Kedourie; Charles Hamilton; June Plaat; Hillel Fradkin; William F. Buckley; Lee Auspitz; Colin Haycraft. Generous financial support was given by the Historical Research Foundation of New York City, and the Lynde and Harry Bradley Foundation of Milwaukee, Wisconsin.

A.J.N.

1

Michael Joseph Oakeshott (1901-90)

Josiah Lee Auspitz

Michael Oakeshott would have enjoyed his funeral. There was almost nothing remarkable about it.

The pelting rain and rough winds that swept the Dorset coast on the morning of December 24 had subsided into a mild blue sky by the early afternoon when the funeral party of a few dozen people converged from several points in England and abroad on the village church at Langton Matravers. The service followed the simplest Anglican rites, and the village pastor, as he likes to be called, began the eulogy sparely, with the dates of the deceased's birth and death, his education, war record, academic career, the names of his surviving family, the thirty-year period of his local residence.

There would have been little more to say, had not the pastor recorded his own astonishment upon opening the *Daily Telegraph* of December 21, 1990, and reading: 'Michael Oakeshott, who has died aged 89, was the greatest political philosopher in the Anglo-Saxon tradition since Mill – or even Burke.' The *Times* the next day brought equally portentous praise: over a sixty-year career of writing and teaching, Oakeshott had done more than anyone this century to make conservatism intellectually respectable. The *Guardian* called him 'perhaps the most original academic political philosopher of this century'. And the *Independent* devoted the better part of a page to an erudite essay on the less overtly political aspects of the philosopher's work, comparing it to that of Montaigne in its 'composure, humour, gentleness, and self-restraint'.

'It appears,' the parson said, 'that we have had a very great man living amongst us.' To verify this he had opened a few of Oakeshott's books, but these, he confessed with a wrinkled brow, would require further study. He consulted instead neighbours, a shopkeeper, a delivery man. They reported that the deceased was a kind man, a cheerful man, very helpful, generous, unpretentious and remarkably youthful. He had a sparkle in his eye, a vigorous gait and a rapport with children, and he drove to Swanage, the nearest town, in his blue MG sports car. Yet no one locally had the slightest idea what the sprightly octogenarian did. His wife, an artist, had a studio in the village, but the philosopher never spoke of his own work.

The parson impressed upon his audience that the Oakeshotts lived modestly in Acton, a cluster of quarry-workers' cottages on the outskirts of the main village. He was struck that so eminent a man should have dwelt in so humble a place. He compared Oakeshott to St Francis, an analogy he found so gripping that he thenceforth referred to the deceased MG-owner as Francis rather than Michael, even as the coffin was lowered into the earth.

As the funeral party walked to the churchyard and thence to the Village Hall for sherry and tea, the philosopher's former colleagues and students from the London School of Economics mingled with his Dorset neighbours, his family and a few old friends. The conversation centered on the lucky change of weather and on Oakeshott himself. At sundown, Christmas Eve, the party dispersed.

His widow returned to their cottage and the visits of kind neighbours, who took with good humour the parson's suggestion that they sat in a hermit's hovel. By Acton standards the Oakeshott cottage was ample, formed of both halves of what had been a two-family house. A small kitchen, dining room and upstairs guest bedroom and bath occupied what had been one dwelling; a living room, study and upstairs bedroom the other. What might have been a second upstairs room had been pulled out to give the living

1. Michael Joseph Oakeshott (1901–1990)

room a two storey skylit space over the fireplace. The wall space that was not covered with book shelves displayed Christel Oakeshott's abstract paintings. In all, the place had more standard amenities than the Oakeshotts' Covent Garden apartment, which had lacked a private bath during most of their residence in London.

The furnishings of the cottage were not so much rude as miscellaneous. The kitchen had two small refrigerators, an old stove, a toaster oven, a space heater and mismatched cabinets. A single piece of carpet, bought at a church rummage sale, covered the floor. Oakeshott had charted the irregular pattern of the appliances and cabinets on the back of the carpet, laid it out in the garden and cut it exactly to fit.

The dishes, cutlery, chairs, rugs and sofas in the house were mostly secondhand, bought at the local flea markets and at the Swanage Oxfam shop where Oakeshott also assembled much of his wardrobe. As a young man he had been a dandy, famous for lecturing in a yellow velvet jacket with a red rose pinned to the lapel. His Dorset attire gave no clue to this past.

A playful touch, a gift from devoted friends, brightened the living room: an antique musical bird cage with a tiny metal lovebird hung in a window facing out onto the garden. The small dining room had just enough space to seat three and house an upright piano, which the Oakeshotts made available to an Acton child for practice.

But the main furnishings of the cottage were Oakeshott's books. He had disposed of most of those he considered merely informative and retained a consummately civilised library. In his later years he took to giving away some of his more cherished volumes, but still there remained shelves upon shelves testifying to years of enjoyment of history and fiction, philosophy and poetry, memoirs and essays, and pleasant hours of browsing in second-hand bookshops. In his last year he re-read the works of one of his favourite Americans, Willa Cather.

Among his personal treasures were an odd assortment marking his own family and education: a Church of England missal translated into Latin, picked up as a curio by his father, a Fabian civil servant; a memorial volume from St George's School, Harpenden, a Quaker-sponsored, progressive, coeducational public school that he had attended during the First World War; a green leather-bound set of Pater's *Marius the Epicurean*, given him as a prize for undergraduate studies at Gonville and Caius College, Cambridge; a carefully annotated paperback copy of Hegel's *Phänomenologie des Geistes* from his university days at Marburg and Tübingen in the mid-twenties, with a batch of notes still tucked into the pages.

A shelf above his desk held the several editions and translations of his own modest output. In all there were two major treatises separated by forty years, the second thoroughly revising the grounds of the first, about two dozen essays collected under overlapping thematic headings, an anthology of political readings, a critical edition and a co-authored book on horse racing.

Though a gracefully bookish man, Oakeshott, as a philosopher, put little trust in the printed word. 'A philosopher is not, as such, a scholar; and philosophy, more often than not, has foundered in learning. There is no book which is indispensable for the study of philosophy. And to speak of a philosopher as ignorant is to commit an *ignoratio elenchi*; an historian or a scientist may be ignorant, philosophers merely stupid.'[1]

Not one of his own books had a proper bibliography. Even his magisterial edition of Hobbes's *Leviathan* contained a list entitled 'Books for Further Reading', which was limited to five modern titles, the most recent being a 1934 work by Leo Strauss. His footnoting was sparse and meant to amplify or amuse rather than to engage in academic diplomacy or display. In scholarly discourse he never rattled off references, affecting instead an English amnesia for the names of works on which he was expert.

Yet when it came to suggesting an apt title, he was like a wise old herbalist dispensing time-tested remedies. If one were working on a problem, he had just the volume to advance one's thinking. If one were going on a trip, he would

---

[1] *Experience and its Modes*, p. 8.

1. Michael Joseph Oakeshott (1901–1990)

present the perfect travel memoir of that place. As a guest, he would rummage around for hours in second-hand bookshops until he found just the right volumes to leave as a present for each member of the family.

Shortly before his death he put into his wife's hands Elinore Pruitt Stewart's memoir of ranching in Wyoming, *Letters of a Woman Homesteader*, which concludes: 'I have tried every kind of work this ranch affords, and I can do any of it. Of course, I am extra strong, but those who try know that strength and knowledge come with doing.' Having done most of the pottering around the house and garden during their thirty years of marriage, Michael also left at his desk a newly acquired Reader's Digest home-repair book, *How to Do Just About Anything*, a title that gently mocked his famous critique of Rationalism.

His knack for prescribing the right book was of a piece with the tact that marked his conversation. Conversation requires entering obliquely into the world of others, and Oakeshott had an uncanny gift for it. He never held forth. He saw conversation not as a scored recitative but as a spontaneously improvised dance in which each participant responds to the movements of the others. A clairvoyance in anticipating the direction of an interlocutor's thought enabled him to enter the flow with gravity or humour, a nod or a monologue, as the rhythm of talk required.

He especially enjoyed conversation with women. In his own generation, this was taken as a mark of unsoundness, or worse, of amorous proclivities. Oakeshott was guilty on both counts. He did love women. And he also took them seriously as intellectuals. The combination was not always happy. Tending to romanticise the capacities of the women he knew, he was bound to suffer occasional disappointments. Should the rare student or colleague in whom he had placed high intellectual hopes turn out to be unexpectedly obtuse, he took it especially hard if the person were female.

A conversation with Oakeshott on philosophy might take many unexpected turns and last for long hours, or might, as he put it in one of his essays, be 'put by for another day but never concluded, ... [with] the participants as playfellows moved, not by a belief in the evanescence of error and imperfection but only by their loyalty and affection for one another.'[2]

'Loyalty and affection for one another' – is the abiding memory of the student who had him for individual tutorial. His normal procedure was to ask the tutee to suggest a writer or a text with which to begin their weekly conversations. If he detected a spark of receptivity to philosophy or history, the two modes of understanding he was intent to teach, all rules were then off. Meetings scheduled for an hour might stretch to two or three. Sometimes the student would be asked to prepare a paper, but not as a regular requirement. Tutor and tutee might prolong the talk for an entire term before the first short essay was assigned.

Oakeshott's lack of assertiveness in these sessions was unfeigned. His view of what he had to teach left little room for eristic. He believed that teaching was also learning. The teacher had to study his pupil, had to attend to the manner as well as to the matter of the lesson. Moreover, 'some activities, like intellectual inquiry, remain always activities of learning'.[3] In a university a tutor and his tutee were both learners, of differing degrees of competence and experience. The aim of a tutorial, as opposed to a lecture, was not to convey organised information, or even to impart a sense of how to interpret and use it, but to bring the student along with oneself to a new level of understanding. Oakeshott's tutees would come away from these sessions without notes but with an example that would, in time, strengthen their appreciation of what Oakeshott called 'the intellectual virtues':

> How does a pupil learn disinterested curiosity, patience, honesty, exactness, industry, concentration and doubt? How does he acquire a sensibility to small differences and the ability to recognize intellectual elegance? How does he come to inherit the disposition to submit to refutation? How does he not merely learn the love of truth and justice, but learn it in such a way as to escape the reproach of

[2] 'The Voice of Poetry in the Conversation of Mankind' in *Rationalism in Politics*, p. 201.
[3] 'Learning and Teaching' in *The Voice of Liberal Learning*, p. 43.

1. Michael Joseph Oakeshott (1901–1990)

fanaticism? And beyond all this there is something more difficult to acquire: namely, the ability to detect the individual intelligence which is at work in every utterance, even those which convey impersonal information ...

The intellectual virtues may be imparted only by a teacher who really cares about them for their own sake, and never stoops to the priggishness of mentioning them. Not the cry but the rising of the wild duck impels the flock to follow him in flight.[4]

Conversation for Oakeshott was not merely the preferred pedagogical method. It was for him the very basis of education, and a metaphor for civilisation itself. Each educational encounter was in its small way an initiation into civilised discourse – into what Dilthey called a *geistige Welt*. The languages of science and mathematics, of arts and letters, of sport, religion, the trades and the professions were all for him part of a 'conversation' that made up the human inheritance. Only in entering this conversation could one become fully human. Education was everywhere the price of entry. For the human birthright consisted not in artifacts but in the modes of intercourse that gave rise to them. These one could possess only by learning them.

The ultimate business of education, then, was learning to be a human being. It might include training in a trade or a skill or a discipline. But to focus on the merely employable or certifiable aspects of education truncated one's vision of human possibility. The teacher, however humble his sphere, had to be understood and respected, and to understand and respect himself, as the agent par excellence of civilisation. 'He may be excused if he finds the present dominant image of civilised life too disagreeable to impart with any enthusiasm to his pupils. But if he has no confidence in any of the standards of worth written into this inheritance of human achievement, he had better not be a teacher; he would have nothing to teach.' The calling of the teacher was neither more nor less than to initiate the pupil into 'the conversation of mankind'.[5]

---

[4] Ibid., pp. 60-2.
[5] Ibid., p. 49.

In Oakeshott's essays, indeed, conversation is presented as 'the appropriate image of human intercourse', and it bears so integral a relation to his person and his practice as to make it also an accessible image with which to approach the more difficult parts of his philosophical work. The notion of conversation sets the tone of his later philosophy, reflects his leading sensibilities and suggests the programme of inquiry he followed.

His view of conversation, like his practice of it, is non-hierarchical, non-directive and non-assertive. In a conversation, as opposed to a disputation, one voice cannot hope to dominate the others. There is no fixed agenda. There is no standard external to the conversation itself by which to judge the utterances made. There is no final point or destination or resolution or decision to be reached:

> In a conversation the participants are not engaged in an inquiry or a debate; there is no 'truth' to be discovered, no proposition to be proved, no conclusion sought. They are not concerned to inform, to persuade, or refute one another, and therefore the cogency of their utterances does not depend upon their all speaking in the same idiom; they may differ without disagreeing. Of course, a conversation may have passages of argument and a speaker is not forbidden to be demonstrative; but reasoning is neither sovereign nor alone, and the conversation itself does not compose an argument.[6]

Conversation is one way of translating – and reinterpreting – the Greek *dialektikê*, which from the earliest times has been seen as central to philosophy. Oakeshott returns it to its most inclusive meaning. In contrast to the two philosophers he first admired, Plato and Hegel, and to Aristotle, upon whom he later came to rely, Oakeshott uses the notion of conversation to demystify philosophy itself. Instead of fastening on 'dialectic' as the aspect of reasoning that places philosophy at the very highest rank, he portrays the philosopher's voice as merely one among many in a broader discourse.

The essence of conversation in his view lies in the

---

[6] *Rationalism in Politics*, p. 198.

1. Michael Joseph Oakeshott (1901–1990)

diversity of voices that may enter into it, and the ability of each to enjoy and acknowledge another without losing its own integrity. The speakers pursue the talk for its own sake, both because they have something serious they want to talk about and because, as human beings, they enjoy the interplay. Philosophy is concerned with the character and limits of each of the voices. It may put its remarks affirmatively or critically, with ardour or resignation, in an appreciative or dyspeptic tone, but it always has the same kind of thing to say: that each voice is less than complete, that its truth to itself, its authenticity, emerges from a specific context, and that there can be discerned in each voice 'languages' that are at once the common heritage of humanity and open to the individual modulations of a given speaker. Because philosophy has no subject matter of its own, it attends only to the conversation itself, listening carefully to each speaker. It is a quintessentially conversable voice because it limits itself to reflecting upon the utterances of the others.

The pace and cadence of Oakeshott's prose harmonise with the conversational image. His writing follows the rhythms of the spoken word without stooping to the colloquial. It presents, at its best, an elevated diction purged of the usual lecture-room tropes. There is rarely an enumeration of essential points to assist the taker of notes, little refutation of other writers, none of the logician's focus on paradox, scant analysis of cases, an absence of jargon. One theme seems to flow effortlessly into another with a subtlety and nuance that may disconcert the reader accustomed to heavier hands: Can any writing this seductive be sound?

And there may be more substantial causes for unease. The image of civilisation as conversation does not clip the wings of philosophy alone. It dissolves also the absolute claims of all other voices. It suggests that each and every human achievement is contingent upon others, that there is no preordained pattern, no standard for human intercourse not already present within it as an inheritance. It thus joins sensibilities not often found in tandem. On one side, it encourages reverence: everything we are and we have we owe to what has come before. On another, it frees the imagination to doubt and to dare: we become what we learn and choose to make of ourselves; our birthright is to find a voice of our own. Oakeshott's union of piety with adventure, tradition with individuality, seriousness with playfulness, reverence with scepticism, affection for human frailty with searing criticism of error is not easily classifiable in twentieth-century philosophy. In a world preoccupied with labels and isms, he defies easy categorisation. To the reader who seeks in philosophy a fixed doctrine or method, his writing seems irritatingly elusive.

Yet undergirding Oakeshott's eloquence and his imagery is a rigorous logical structure of his own composition. to make place for a conversational sensibility, he reworks the way in which Western philosophy takes account of variety in experience. In so doing, he has left his mark on a central category: modality.

'Modality,' F.H. Bradley observed, 'is not an alluring theme.' Like critical philosophy generally, it lacks substantive content. Modal distinctions are the philosopher's way of dealing with variety without invoking facts, natural kinds, individuals or classes. One does not speak of the Golden Delicious, the Granny Smith and the McIntosh as modes of an apple, though they are varieties. But one does speak of modes of perceiving, cognising or eating an apple, modes of being, modes of judgment, modes of the syllogism, modes of the musical scale, modes of transport and grammatical moods, a variant of modes. Modes mark the line at which judgmental distinctions are treated as differences of kind rather than degree. Modes do not take up time or space, though there may be temporal and spatial modes. Modal distinctions are compossible rather than mutually exclusive. Like the voices in Oakeshott's conversation, they may coexist without conflicting.

To speak of a mode is not simply to notice variety, but to insert some active principle of mind into the discussion of it. Modal distinctions follow some pattern, rule, or order that is the product of human intelligence. It is for this reason that Hegel rejected Spinoza's view of intellect and extension as

1. Michael Joseph Oakeshott (1901–1990)

the two universal modes (*Modi*) of substance: since the notion of modality already presupposes a world mediated by mind, intellect cannot be *modally* coequal with extension. And it is for the same reason that philosophers hewing to a strictly empiricist line studiously avoid the category except in its narrowest technical usages within logic.

Oakeshott's first book, *Experience and its Modes*, proposed a conception of modality that has stamped his thinking ever since. He summarised the theme for the dust jacket of the first paperback edition in 1985 (the 1933 and 1966 hardback editions of one thousand copies each having been sold out):

> Modality: human experience recognised as a variety of independent, self-consistent worlds of discourse, each the invention of human intelligence, but each also to be understood as abstract and an arrest in human experience. The theme is pursued in a consideration of the practical, the historical and the scientific modes of understanding.

Oakeshott's usage is unusual in restricting modality to 'self-consistent worlds of discourse' or (in the book itself) 'worlds of ideas'. A mode for him is not, as it has been for most philosophers, a general principle of differentiation; it is a coherent construct, a world unto itself that portrays the world at large under a set of abstractions peculiar to itself. Thus, science is a way of looking at the entire world through a limited set of (mainly quantitative) ideas. A similar pattern of abstractions defines history, practical activity and, in a later essay, poetry.

The philosopher's role is to discern the leading ideas that each mode postulates. Much as an accomplished portraitist evokes a human face with a few strokes, Oakeshott captures the organising abstractions of a mode of human discourse.

This he originally conceived as an idealist enterprise inspired by Hegel, who saw the business of the philosophical sciences as 'the derivation and cognition of ... particular modes (*Weisen*)'. Similar efforts in this century can be found in the delineation of 'forms' of the spirit by Collingwood and Croce. Unlike these two writers, Oakeshott refuses to give any ranking to the modes. He declines to put philosophy at the top of a scale, with history and science below. He also severs philosophy radically from the history of it. Though much of his work was devoted to the history of political thought, he considered the activity of being a historian modally distinct from philosophical reflection proper. The philosopher makes use of a tradition of inquiry, but for him it is timeless, present in his imagination as a store of examples and suggestions. Oakeshott followed his first university lecturer in philosophy, McTaggart, in excluding the dimension of time from a purely philosophical criterion.

Yet in other respects Oakeshott's approach betrays his early academic training as a historian. (An undergraduate degree in history was his only formal certification.) His distinctive use of modality transposes to a philosophical idiom the historian's everyday practice in identifying persistent patterns of thought and action. A history of an architectural style, for example, or of a literary genre, an institution, or a political doctrine depends upon identifying a shifting but relatively stable set of characteristics that compose an identity (the baroque, the novel, the modern university, Rationalism). Oakeshott's modes raise such characteristics to the level of a coherent ideal construct. They set forth patterns that have achieved a logical as opposed to a merely circumstantial or doctrinal integrity. Oakeshott concedes that his modes have developed historically. Their interest to philosophy, however, consists in their having achieved an 'ideal character' that may be sketched without reference to time and place.

He recognises a limited number of self-consistent modes: at first, science, history and practice; later, in *The Voice of Poetry in the Conversation of Mankind* (1959), 'poetry', which stands for aesthetic experience generally; still later, in *On Human Conduct* (1975), he revises his terms to recognise 'modes of association' in practical life, of which the most notable is 'civil association' or the rule of non-instrumental law. (This fulfilled a project laid out in his first extended discussion of law, 'The Concept of a Philosophical Jurisprudence', which appeared in 1938.) In *On History and Other Essays* (1983) he returns to the discussion of the historical mode and to the rule of law – two topics on which

1. Michael Joseph Oakeshott (1901–1990)

his work, spanning half a century, will not soon be surpassed.

Each of his modes is a systematic composition of ideas. One might, following Locke, call them complex as opposed to simple modes. They correspond to only one of the terms Hegel uses for modality, *Weise*, as opposed to *Modus*. The German *Weise* suggests a way or *manner* of thought and action, and this captures exactly Oakeshott's intention. A mode for him qualifies the world 'adverbially'; it modifies on-going activity, enabling us to experience the world historically, practically, scientifically, poetically, as we choose. In the conversational metaphor, the modes are the 'voices' by which we can develop our own way of speaking.

Though Oakeshott's portrayal of modality as a world of discourse shares the concern with language common among philosophers in the English-speaking world, it contains a speculative dimension lacking in the (largely Viennese) fashions that came to dominate the post-war Anglo-American mainstream. It leaps beyond the method of 'concrete cases'; Oakeshott cannot examine a case without enquiring into the organising ideas that are presupposed in recognising it as a case. And since Oakeshott's modes define their own standards of truth and relevance, they rule out the view that language is meaningful only if it is 'falsifiable' with respect to some external reality; the reality to which a mode refers is always internal to it.

Oakeshott's philosophical gift is connoisseurial rather than analytic. He identifies the provenance and excellences of each mode, and within it distinguishes what is generic from what is merely incidental. This requires a systematic intelligence, but one weighted toward *l'esprit de finesse* rather than *l'esprit géométrique*. Oakeshott has a philosophical discernment akin to the practical acumen that makes someone a good judge of character. He fastens on the ideal character of whatever comes his way, distinguishing what is coherent and enduring from what is merely idiosyncratic.

This same capacity carries over to his non-philosophical writing. In his studies of political thought, his reviews, and even his polemical essays, he is able with great dispatch to enter into thought remote from his own, give an account of it on its own terms, and evoke the unstated sensibilities that it conveys. His discussions of individual writers are exemplary for exposing the underlying logical structure and pinpointing organising concepts.

An especially influential example is to be found in a book of readings first issued in January 1939 entitled *The Social and Political Doctrines of Contemporary Europe*. It contained original texts for the doctrines of Representative Democracy (or Liberalism rightly considered), Catholicism, Communism, Fascism, and National Socialism. Oakeshott selects texts that let each doctrine speak for itself, with one exception. Hitler at that time permitted only an expurgated version of *Mein Kampf* to be translated into English, and the German publisher would not allow the Leader's fundamental tenets to be translated in Oakeshott's reader. In the absence of direct quotation, Oakeshott provided 'Some Notes on the Doctrines of *Mein Kampf*', a précis of the systematic elements of Nazism – its theories of race, blood, leadership and individuality – that 'separate it firmly from every other current doctrine'.

Oakeshott's few published writings on religion (and, as he early considered taking a degree in theology, there are doubtless unpublished materials as well) give further evidence of his eye for the way in which ideas hang together. He would appear to have viewed Western Christianity as having achieved a flexible ideal character that made the historical element dispensable, philosophical rationales irrelevant, many dogmas open to radical reinterpretation, but certain images, such as the Fall and the Crucifixion, essential in some form to its doctrines of consolation, moral responsibility and divine love.

That Oakeshott should have become known as a political philosopher says more about the cast of the twentieth century than of his own mind. He appears to address politics mainly because it displays the most egregious of the confusions he wishes to dispel. The word *politics* does not appear in the body of his first book, which presents religion as the epitome of 'practice'. But the view of modality that he

1. Michael Joseph Oakeshott (1901–1990)

develops puts him on a collision course with modern political rhetoric. If practice is modally distinct from science, history, philosophy and poetry, it follows that a politics which purports to be derived from scientific, historical, philosophical or aesthetic truths is fraudulent. Oakeshott is unflinching in drawing out this conclusion. He dwells not on the easy targets – Nazi racial theory, dialectical materialism, the mythic claptrap of the Italian futurists and Fascists – but on the attempts to ground democracy in self-evident philosophical truths, to root religion in theories of nature and history or, indeed, to put any activity on a rationalised basis.

He lets his criticisms fall where they may. The founders of the American republic, whose political wisdom he admired, are faulted for their excessive rationalism. Augustine, whose Christianity is perhaps closest to Oakeshott's own, is footnoted in tandem with Trotsky for the error of seeing in history a design with practical bearings. Hayek and others with whom he sympathises on matters of policy are criticised for making a theoretical fetish out of an ideal of freedom.

As Oakeshott sees it, ideological excess is deeply embedded in Western Christianity and thence in modern thought. The conditions under which Christianity became a proselytising religion in its first four centuries gave undue prominence to a 'morality of ideals' over a morality of custom and habit. Organised for conversion, Christendom was prone to mistake moralising for morals. When in modern times its ingrained weakness for creeds combined with the vocabulary of modern science, a new die was cast. Rationalism emerged on the scene.

Rationalism consists in an exaggerated faith in what is technical, premediated, rationalisable, and (in its misreading of the mode) scientific. It recognises only articulated as opposed to tacit forms of knowledge. It views the world as a series of problems to be solved by direct means and the application of the most advanced knowledge. In politics it supports the demand for a theoretically grounded ideology; in morals, for explicit ideals deduced from nature; in education, for vocational training in the techniques rather than the languages and modes of civilised discourse. The past four centuries have, according to Oakeshott, been especially favourable to its growth. The enfranchisement of new classes, the establishment of new nations, the rise of new industries demanding trained workers, a mobile and expanding population – such factors give rise to 'new men' seeking an abridgment of tradition, looking for quick answers, preferring progress to precedent and often deeply resentful of the individuality they have not had the leisure to cultivate. Rationalism is a syndrome Oakeshott describes, deplores and accepts as an enduring element in modern Western thought.

Its dominance is evident in 'the politics of the felt need', which afflicts parties of both Left and Right. When politicians speak of the need to solve social problems and see the aim of the state as policy, or planning, or national purpose, they fall into the language of Rationalism, regardless of the substantive content of their prescriptions. Oakeshott has no direct remedy – the search for direct remedies is, after all, a rationalist trait. But in essays and reviews published between 1947 and 1949 in the *Cambridge Journal*, which he also edited, he does focus on three countermeasures to abate the worst excesses. The first is the dispersion of power to limit the monopolistic appetites of the state, the labour unions and large corporations. The second is adherence to the rule of law, which guarantees the rights of property and association that enable people to pursue self-chosen rather than collectively imposed visions of the good. The third is an insistence on a spacious view of education, in opposition to the rationalist's narrow focus on manpower training and civic indoctrination.

Oakeshott's anti-Rationalist essays have a polemical edge that his work loses after the immediate post-war years. He was concerned to draw a firm line between wartime thinking and civilian life. At other times his interest in current political affairs quickens only when they touch on the university.

In 1951, when he succeeded Harold Laski as Professor of Political Science, the London School of Economics was not the most congenial place for a man of his views. It had been

1. Michael Joseph Oakeshott (1901–1990)

founded by the Fabians, Oakeshott's father among them, as a trade school for a new governing class. Undergraduates from all over the world had flocked there in the expectation of learning exactly what Oakeshott averred could not be taught. Like a pacifist at a military academy, an anti-Rationalist at the London School of Economics had to give an account of himself.

All the more so since Oakeshott's chair carried with it the chairmanship of the Department of Government. For fifteen years, until the London School of Economics moved to three-year rotating chairmanships, Oakeshott ran the department. By all accounts he presided over an era of good feeling unusual in large academic departments devoted to politics. But he still had to answer the question of what it was, given his views, he presumed to teach.

His response was to reaffirm in a ringing series of essays the liberal character of the university. 'Greed or the desire to appear abreast of the times' often led universities to accept chairs dedicated to negligible topics. The political interests of the dons themselves, many of whom had been seconded into government, led them to devote courses to their current projects. 'But if every don were to teach undergraduates what he himself is interested in, and if every professorial chair were held to entail or to authorise a counterpart to itself in undergraduate education, there would be little in these days to distinguish a university from a mad-house.'[7]

What universities could teach about politics, he said, is no different from what they could teach generally: the explanatory modes of discourse – science, history, and philosophy – and the intellectual virtues that might be imparted with them. The study of politics, therefore, had to use that topic as an occasion for initiating students into these modes. Happily, in two of them, history and philosophy, there was a literature serviceable to the task.

When Oakeshott retired in 1969 he devoted himself to further contributions to this literature.

---

[7] 'The Study of Politics in a University' in *Rationalism in Politics*, p. 330n.

It was in that year that I first met him. I came not as his student or colleague but as an admiring, dissatisfied reader of *Experience and its Modes*. The book suggested questions about the character of practical knowledge that could not be addressed without violating its own modal categories. If science and history were categorially distinct from practice, how were we to describe the way in which, for example, case histories and scientific research inform the practice of medicine? His critique of Rationalism seemed to me to sidestep this question; it exposed the abuses of technical knowledge without providing a nuanced philosophical vocabulary with which to discuss its intelligent use. Conversely, there was the problem of the practical aspect of science and history. Were not scientists and historians practitioners of their disciplines and to that extent also in the practical mode? And if science, history and philosophy all had an explanatory or theoretical character that made them fit for a liberal university, did they not all in this sense partake of a common practice of inquiry that blurred the modal distinctions among them? I visited him in his office to air these questions, and I returned a year and a half later for a longer discussion.

Such issues had occurred to him as well. He was working on a book that would, among other things, deal with them. A correspondence developed. In 1974 when he came to America for a lecture he asked if my wife and I had an extra bed to break the monotony of academic guest suites. A year later, on another such trip, he again spent a few days with us. Everyone in our family had the benefit of his conversation.

When *On Human Conduct* appeared in 1975, I already knew from his letters the refinements that would resolve the anomalies of the earlier book. He now treated any settled activity as a practice, so that he could speak of the practice of history or of science or of theorising generally. The coherence of each of the explanatory modes he now rooted in the order of inquiry pursued: science inquires into a world seen in terms of processes, history in terms of contingent conduct, philosophy in terms of the conditionality of experience generally. He was thus able to retain the

1. Michael Joseph Oakeshott (1901–1990)

integrity of the several 'voices' in civilisation in a way that gave more scope to the interplay of the modes. The greater suppleness of this approach also enabled him him to accept a limited role for 'theorem-making' (or what the Poles and others call praxiology) within the non-theoretical practices. In all, he now had the basis for a conspectus of modes of theorising.

But what I had not anticipated was an extension of his concept of modality into the arena of law. Oakeshott's eye for ideal character had discerned a 'small composition of related ideas' in the emergence of the states of modern Europe, and in philosophical reflection upon them. He called this composition 'the civil condition' and the form of human relations it specified 'civil association'. This denoted not a doctrine or a political tendency, but a self-contained mode of association more commonly called the rule of law. As a modal complex it could be detached from historical contingency and understood philosophically in terms of a few organising ideas.

Much as an explanatory mode like science or history defines its own standards of truth and relevance, a legal system defines its own sphere. It is a self-consistent and self-authenticating world in which law (*lex*) serves as a language of civil intercourse among citizens (*cives*) in accordance with a set of public conditions (*respublica*). Oakeshott uses Latin terms for such matters to create a technical vocabulary (his first attempt at jargon) to distance his discussion from everyday political rhetoric. He uses the terms *civil* and *civility* in the root sense to pertain to citizenship. And he limits the word *politics* to the activity within civil association of debating the desirability of *lex*.

His civil association is thus neither an empirical generalisation nor a prescription for action but a leap of philosophical imagination to define the minimal conditions for a rule of law regime. Oakeshott shows that the postulates of civility are few. Democracy is not among them; nor is the free market, an economy, a bill of rights, standing armies, a monopoly of police forces, an executive branch, a national parks system, a civil service, foreign policy, or indeed any policy, religious belief, old-age pensions, stable families, public schools, modern sewage treatment, rockets to Mars, divine justice, natural law, or the salute to the flag. Such things may be desiderata from many points of view, to be debated and legislated upon in civil politics, but they are not defining features of civil association as such.

All the rule of law requires is a body of formal equals who understand the law as authoritative, recognise an obligation to comply with it, and subscribe to procedures for enacting, amending and interpreting it.

Moral restraint, not conceptual parsimony, prompts Oakeshott to apply Ockham's razor to the rule of law. Unlike other modes, the legal system is compulsory. Its subjects are human beings most of whom fall under it by accident of birth. They have an obligation to comply with disagreeable laws, even as they try to amend them. The law presumes to define their personhood, to lay down the conditions of its own authority, and to specify the procedures by which they may appeal to this authority. Any excess in the definition of what is essential to it, therefore, opens the door to unexamined abuse, or worse, moral enormity.

Oakeshott's is the first philosophical definition successfully to relieve the rule of law from reliance on the category of purpose, to show that civil association has a different logic from that of everyday life. As individual human beings, Oakeshott tells us, we are full of projects, plans, policies and purposes. Collectively, we may pursue these in a variety of institutions – in 'enterprise association', as he calls it. But civil association is modally distinct from this: *cives* accept not a set of common aims but a commonly recognised system of rules. As with the English language, which facilitates each of our projects, grows with them, but cannot be adequately explained as an instrument for getting them done, civility has a purely procedural integrity independent of the purposes that this or that law may seem to serve at this or that time. Its conditions are not substantive but adverbial, enabling us to conduct ourselves 'civilly' throughout our many enterprises.

Civil associates may, at choice, enter into relationships of

1. Michael Joseph Oakeshott (1901–1990)

affection, of discourse, of gainful enterprise, or of playful engagement, but in respect of being civilly associated they cannot be either required or forbidden to do so; they are required only to subscribe to the conditions of *respublica* ... In short, the civil condition and a state understood in terms of civil association postulates self-determined autonomous human beings seeking the satisfaction of their wants in self-chosen transactions with others of their kind.

Civil association, then, requires a spirit of indirection that must be widely diffused. It presupposes human beings with purposes, plans, and projects of their own who recognise the law as not sharing these. It requires of them a non-managerial, non-anthropomorphic view of the state. For it follows from Oakeshott's modal categories that to the extent that the state is understood as a civil association, without human personality and without purposes, plans, and projects of its own, *cives* shall have unfettered conditions under which to choose their versions of human personality.

That civil association as an 'ideal character' can exist only in compromised form does not diminish the force of this argument. On the contrary, it suggests a programme of fine discrimination among the varieties of state action, and renewed attention to the ideal and literature of the *Rechtstaat*.

In the fifteen years that remained to him after the publication of *On Human Conduct*, Oakeshott stayed in England, spending more and more time in Dorset and finally giving up his London apartment altogether. He had a further book to finish, *On History and Other Essays*. It contains some of his most sure-handed and well-balanced philosophical writing. He had declared early that 'philosophy has less place for what is second-class than any other field of intellectual endeavour', and this slim volume is a fitting endpaper to his youthful aspirations.

A piece entitled 'The Rule of Law' puts into crisper form his definition of civil association and adds a discussion of justice ('the *jus* of *lex*'). As a lighter counterpoint, a midrashic retelling of 'The Tower of Babel' turns the biblical tale into an anti-utopian allegory of enterprise association.

Three essays on historiography form the core of the collection. They take up the discussion of history as a mode that Oakeshott began in 1933. If R.G. Collingwood was correct in calling that earlier effort 'the high water mark of English thought upon history', the essays published fifty years later must be the flood tide. They move with Oakeshott's usual elegance and economy to deflate the leading pretensions.

The central essay treats the category of relation appropriate in the writing of history. Oakeshott rejects 'the fortuitous, the causal, the similar, the correlative, the analogous' in favour of 'the contingent'. He suggests that historians can explain events only in terms of antecedent events that 'touch' them. By this he means that the antecedent events that the historian notices must make a significant difference in shaping the subsequent. The evidence is only nominally 'the past'. What historians really do is make certain kinds of inference from the present – from documents, artifacts, and other survivals that are available when they write. The inferential relations are designed not to support an argument but to show how one event is best explained in terms of others that bear upon it.

The Purbeck region of Dorset, rich in quarries, provides him with his most telling image: the dry wall, in which the stones are held together by their shapes without premeditated design. 'It is what its components, in touching, constitute.' There is no mortar for the historian – no laws of history, no necessity of events, no grand design, organic growth, divine purpose, national destiny, permanent essence, teleological unfolding. The historian has no set rules, only the exercise of judgment in relating human events to others in a continuous chain of contiguities. Locale may make a significant difference for one event but not for another, and the same holds for any other factor. The only constant in history is human conduct itself, always unpredictable, always open to intelligent choice.

The response to this book, as to *On Human Conduct*, spared him too hectic a retirement. The reprinting of *Experience and its Modes* and the consequent demand upon

1. Michael Joseph Oakeshott (1901–1990)

him for two sentences on the dust jacket might be attributed to interest stirred by the essays on history. But otherwise, the world did not beat a path to his door. He sat for a portrait to be hung at his old Cambridge college, cooperated with the authors of two books and a thesis written on his work, attended a reunion of his Second World War unit, 'Phantom' (an intelligence group that made reports from the front), took an occasional trip to London, accepted a few honours, attended the odd conference, kept up with his correspondents, wrote letters of recommendation, made aphoristic entries in a notebook, dusted and reshelved his books, pottered about in the garden, and entertained a few house guests.

From time to time I was one of these. I last visited him the summer before his death. I was on my way home from a philosophy conference in Poland, a country where the late attempt to organise the state as an enterprise association will give many readers instant rapport with the translation of Oakeshott's work in preparation by the former underground publisher, Respublica Press. He came in his little blue MG to fetch me from the station.

We arrived in time for tea, which was Christel's speciality. Michael did all of the heavier meals, she the lighter ones. During this stay Michael insisted on preparing all the dinners at home. He was an excellent short-order cook who made imaginative use of ready-made and local ingredients. His soups were tasty combinations of French and Swiss powdered varieties; his sauces likewise. He took care that the four main meals alternated beef, veal, chicken, and fish. The chicken, as I recall, was served with pasta and the Italian flag colours of pepper – green, yellow and red. The dessert that night was strawberries with a cointreau-flavoured vanilla ice cream made locally at Corfe Castle.

He was the most considerate host. This time, he had saved for me a clipping of a long review of the early works of C.S. Peirce. He knew that in pursuing the problem of modality I had become interested in Peirce's work, which I found rich in approaches lacking in his own. He also put in my hands Sarah Orne Jewett's *Country of the Pointed Firs*, a memoir of Maine that he joined Willa Cather in admiring.

Its words (p. 46) about hospitality applied to Oakeshott as well:

> Her hospitality was something exquisite; she had the gift, which so many women lack, of being able to make themselves and their houses belong entirely to a guest's pleasure, – that charming surrender for the moment of themselves and whatever belongs to them, so that they make a part of one's own life that can never be forgotten. Tact is after all a kind of mind-reading, and my hostess had the golden gift. Sympathy is of the mind as well as the heart.

He showed me also a few recent things on his own work that I had not seen: a new Japanese translation of *Rationalism in Politics*, a Harvard PhD thesis, a book of essays – *The Activity of Politics* – by a promising young scholar, and the clippings of four reviews of his collected essays on education.

We did a tour of the garden. He was wearing the yellow sweater he had worn in a photograph sent the previous fall of himself flanked by two towering sunflowers. He had planted many more sunflowers this year. The laburnum had been blown over and needed to be restaked and tied down. We did this together. He showed me the improvements he had made in the shed since my last stay.

The rest of the visit was spent walking, talking, reading and viewing Christel's drawings and paintings. Michael was alert to European affairs. How long would it take the Poles to free themselves economically from the Russians? What was Budapest like these days? And what about the coming re-unification of Germany? He had misgivings about locating the new capital in Berlin. His abiding interest, however, was people. He kept track of many friends and their children, and of his two grandsons as well. He was especially interested in those who had ventured off the beaten paths. Through his memories, I had been introduced to a gallery of adventurous characters, a few of whom I met for the first time at his funeral, more of whom were either dead or in faraway places. I had heard most about his teachers, whose idiosyncrasies he dwelled upon with affection.

In years past, he had joined me on long walks along the

1. Michael Joseph Oakeshott (1901–1990)

seacoast. On this visit he accompanied me only to the first stile and dry wall at the edge of Acton. At night he apologised in advance that he might be up with a catarrh. He had tried all sorts of patent medicines for it and had even given up smoking. When I mentioned that my grandfather had had the same problem and had given up cigarettes at ninety-three, Michael grew wide-eyed. Ninety-three! What an age! Christel reminded him that he was not so far from that age himself.

One morning he excused himself to go into Swanage for a medical checkup. It was only after his death that I learned, as did Christel, that these were weekly trips for cancer treatments.

A letter from him six weeks later was written in a slightly scrawled deviation from his usual precise script. He confessed to being in pain. His wife noticed something unusual when for two days in mid-December he failed to rise early to make the fire. He died in his bed around midnight on December 18/19, just a week after his eighty-ninth birthday.

In re-reading some of his writings after his death, I noticed that I had marked an aside in an essay on history that poses further questions about his view of modality. He says that the 'universe of practical discourse' may be seen 'in terms of moral (that is, non-instrumental) considerations and compunctions but not in the poetic terms of affection, friendship, and love which belong to another world'.

Elsewhere he identified the poetic mode as a world of images contemplated for the sheer delight of them. Placing 'affection, friendship and love' in this modality suggests that the line between fact and fiction is irrelevant in such matters. I had meant to ask him about that.

2

A Choice and Master Spirit

Russell Price

I knew Michael Oakeshott for nearly thirty years. At first, he was my graduate supervisor, then our relationship was gradually transformed into friendship; for the last fifteen years we were on first-name terms. After I left London, in September 1964, we met occasionally, and corresponded from time to time. He read most of my work on Machiavelli (though he professed not to be 'a proper Machiavelli scholar', he had a remarkable understanding of his thought) and on other subjects, and, like many other scholars, I am greatly indebted to him for numerous perceptive hints and valuable suggestions. Generosity was one of his outstanding qualities, and he was never so busy with his own work that he could not spare the time for a careful reading of other people's manuscripts.

As with many others, I suppose, the first piece of his that I read was the Introduction to his edition of Hobbes's *Leviathan*, when I was studying the history of political thought at the University of Wellington, in the mid-1950s. A little later, I read his famous essays on 'Rationalism in Politics' and 'Rational Conduct', as well as his inaugural lecture on 'Political Education'. I was also very impressed by his pre-War volume, *The Social and Political Doctrines of Contemporary Europe*, the short introduction to which seemed to treat very authoritatively the essential features of the ideologies and doctrines that then flourished. All these pieces were beautifully written; moreover, they

2. A Choice and Master Spirit

revealed a mind of great distinction, very incisive and discerning, and they displayed a wide learning in various intellectual fields. Oakeshott was very far from being a narrow specialist, and this also greatly appealed to me. It seemed entirely appropriate that he should have been the editor of that wide-ranging and excellent monthly (alas, rather short-lived), the *Cambridge Journal*, and not of some professional journal. His writings were very stimulating, and opened up vistas that seemed very well worth exploring. I noted, too, Collingwood's judgment, in *The Idea of History*, that the chapter on history in Oakeshott's *Experience and its Modes* represented the high-water mark of English thought on historical writing and its philosophical problems.

After graduating in politics and history, and teaching politics for two years, I aspired to undertake further studies overseas, and applied to the London School of Economics to study Hume's political thought under Michael Oakeshott; I had the good fortune to be accepted, and arrived in England late in September 1962. On my first day, I walked from my lodgings in Hampstead to the centre of London, and visited the LSE. I had always been a little disappointed and puzzled that such an eminent man should have published no books during the eleven years in which he had held the Chair of Political Science. Arriving at the windows of the Economists Bookshop, I was excited to see displayed a copy of *Rationalism in Politics and Other Essays*, which had just been published. Going inside, I discovered that it contained some new essays, as well as those that I had read with such pleasure. I soon bought the book and read it carefully; although some passages seemed obscure or unpersuasive, altogether it struck me as a remarkably impressive volume, and I read with keen interest the reviews of it that began to appear in various weeklies.

Soon I made an appointment to meet my new supervisor. When I entered his book-lined study, I was rather surprised to find his secretary, Miss West, sitting at a small desk near the window. Michael Oakeshott was sitting at a larger desk; he rose and greeted me warmly. He looked much younger than his sixty years. He had a fine head, plentiful straight light-brown hair, untouched by grey, and his slightly sallow face was completely unlined. Only pronounced rings (or incipient bags) under his eyes hinted at his real age.

Indeed, Oakeshott remained youthful-looking for several more years; only as he approached his mid-seventies did his hair turn grey and become thinner, and after that he showed no further obvious signs of ageing. I did not see him between 1979 (shortly afterwards he left London, and moved permanently to his Dorset cottage) and 1988, when we both attended a History of Ideas Colloquium at Durham University; I found him scarcely changed in appearance.

Oakeshott was not tall (about 5′ 7″ or 5′ 8″, I suppose, which must have been roughly the average height for an Englishman of his generation); but he was slim, and I was not conscious of any lack of height until several years later, when we were standing and chatting with one of my colleagues who was over six feet. His voice was light, slightly high-pitched, and his clothes had a kind of informal elegance; he was wearing a brown corduroy jacket. I thought he looked very distinguished.

He was very friendly, smiled frequently and occasionally chuckled in a slightly mischievous way. He inquired after two New Zealanders, Peter Munz (whom he had known at Cambridge) and John Pocock, whose work he greatly admired. Indeed, he seemed to entertain a flatteringly high opinion of New Zealand students; afterwards, it occurred to me that he would have tended to meet the better ones. He appeared to have plenty of time for conversation and for discussing my future studies; then, as always, he never gave the impression that he was pressed for time and had other things to attend to.

Michael Oakeshott's manner was always modest and unassuming; he was completely lacking in self-importance. I found him to be less formidable than I had expected; he expressed his ideas rather tentatively, with a very slight stammer, and there were some pauses. He smoked a couple of cigarettes rather thoughtfully, and once or twice got up from his chair and, with his head bent slightly forward (in a way that I later found to be very characteristic), searched for a book that would shed light on some point we were discussing.

In fact Oakeshott's contributions to conversations and, especially, to intellectual discussions, would often be a mixture of pauses and a flow of interesting ideas. I would not say that fluent oral exposition was his forte; I am not quite sure why, because he obviously had a very good mind, and a very quick one, too. But it was also a very subtle mind, and perhaps he was unduly conscious of the ambiguity or complexity of ideas, and the qualifications that needed to be made to almost any statement, and this led to hesitations when speaking. Whatever the reason for this may have been, his written judgments, whether expounding his own views or criticising those of others, were usually strikingly confident and decisive. He was a very polished, stylish lecturer, and his lectures (delivered from very full notes) were invariably well constructed, and interesting in content. I do not think that he had ever studied voice production: he raised his voice sufficiently to be heard by everyone in the Old Theatre, but he did not project it forcefully or vary his tone very much; perhaps he disdained any oratorical devices. I am inclined to think that it was in his writings that Oakeshott's distinctive talents were manifested to greatest advantage.

Nevertheless, I think that, in supervising sessions, there was another reason for his tentativeness: his desire not to be too forceful, not to impose his ideas on others, especially on research students, who should be expected to work out most things for themselves, with a little help from him. He wanted to suggest some possible lines of thought, which might prove fruitful, but certainly not to formulate a plan that a researcher should follow. And this approach was admirable, it seems to me. He was a very good supervisor. He was exceedingly generous with his time, and one knew that one's work would always receive a very careful reading from him. He would produce a page or two of comments: doubts about this point or that, matters that he thought needed clarification or further development, and one or two new ideas might be suggested. His comments were almost always about matters of substance rather than style (at least, this was so with my work).

The same care and generosity were apparent in his

reviewing, and over the years he reviewed many books. He was an exacting critic, concerned with pointing out obscurities and weaknesses, but he was never niggling, and was always appreciative of the merits of books. He was an excellent reviewer: his critical notice of J.D. Mabbott's *The State and The Citizen*,[1] and his reviews of J.R. Lucas's *The Principles of Politics*[2] and J.C. Holt's *Magna Carta*[3] are fine examples of his thoughtful, sympathetic and penetrating reviewing. Another characteristic of his reviews was his habit of beginning by placing the book under review in a wide context. Indeed, this was a feature of all his work, and reflects not only his broad scholarship but his constant concern to relate the particular to the general, one topic to another, to emphasise the connectedness of things: in short, to consider subjects in a properly philosophical way. Thus his essay on 'The Study of "Politics" in a University', after some introductory remarks, begins by considering education in general, and then the proper character of a university education, before dealing with the 'appropriate' ways of studying Politics.

Another conspicuous characteristic of Oakeshott was his remarkable energy, both physical and intellectual. He came to Lancaster to read a paper on 'The Civil Condition', in March 1972, when he had just turned seventy. The paper was at four o'clock, but he wanted to come early so that he could see the University, which he had never visited. I picked him up at the station shortly after one. We did a tour of the city, which he enjoyed seeing, in my car. Then we walked all round the University: he wanted to see the Library, the Indoor Recreation Centre (where he watched with interest various sporting activities), and also some of the Colleges (at one of which he stopped to talk to a former LSE student whom he had recognised). A lengthy discussion followed his paper, during which he responded well to questions; then there were drinks and general conversation. Afterwards our party went to a hotel for dinner, at which he was in very good form. We conversed

[1] *Mind*, Vol.LVIII (1949), pp. 378-89.
[2] *Political Studies*, Vol. XV (1967), pp. 224-7.
[3] *Government and Opposition*, Vol. 1 (1965-6), pp. 266-71.

2. A Choice and Master Spirit

about all kinds of topics until well after midnight. Next morning I drove him to Preston Station. (As we approached Preston, he mentioned that, after graduating, he had taught at the Lytham St Anne's Grammar School for a couple of years.) In Preston, the heavy Saturday morning traffic somewhat delayed us. Although we arrived a good five minutes before his train was due to depart, he was obviously nervous about missing it (he always made a point of being punctual, though he once told me that at Cambridge he didn't use a watch), and he almost ran to the platform. During his visit, he had displayed extraordinary stamina for an old man. Though of slight build, he obviously possessed a wiry strength. In 1988 he was still capable of rapid movement. At the Durham Colloquium, one of the sessions was just about to begin when he entered the crowded room; someone across the room gave up his seat, and he walked towards it swiftly. On the previous afternoon I had noticed him walking very slowly along a street, and looking downwards. I thought sadly: Michael has finally slowed down. But after observing the swift walk, I concluded that the pavement must have been uneven, and that he had just been walking very carefully.

Oakeshott's intellectual energy was even more impressive. The fruits of his long retirement were two important new books (two other volumes, containing older work, were also published during this period), and several essays and reviews. Although he no longer wrote for publication after *On History* appeared in 1983, until his last short illness he was always reading and thinking, and writing letters. He remained a student (in the fullest sense of the word) until the end of a very long life. At the Durham Colloquium, when he was eighty-six, at times (unsurprisingly) he seemed rather old and tired; but he was in excellent form when he chaired Quentin Skinner's lecture on Hobbes and liberty. His introduction was typically graceful and witty (Skinner was 'an *éminence* not yet *grise*'), and when the discussion was going in a way that he obviously found unsatisfactory, he intervened himself, addressing three or four sharp questions to Skinner.

His intellectual energy went together with (or, perhaps,

partly manifested itself in) a tendency to become somewhat dissatisfied with his earlier treatment of subjects (despite all the time and care he had expended on them). He was always prepared to engage in some new thinking about old subjects.

Perhaps the most striking example of this is the way he kept returning to the philosophical problems raised by historical writing. (He eschewed the word 'historiography' in *On History*, perhaps unwisely, because I think the distinction between 'history' – in the sense of 'what happened in the past' – and 'historical writing' sometimes became blurred.) After a lengthy treatment of this subject in his first book, *Experience and its Modes* (1933), he returned to it in the 1950s in his fairly long essay, 'The Activity of being an Historian'; and, once more, from his early seventies, he devoted most of his last completely new book, *On History and Other Essays*, to re-examining the same topic.

This determination to see if he could express his views in a more satisfactory way was admirable; most old men are understandably reluctant to undertake the arduous task of re-thinking a subject or of forging a new vocabulary. In his memorial address at the LSE, Kenneth Minogue quoted a remarkably candid and moving passage from a letter in which Oakeshott explained that the composition of *On Human Conduct* was proceeding much more slowly than he had expected, and that he had felt obliged to fashion a new vocabulary in order to deal with the problems he had encountered; but he didn't know whether it might not yet fall to pieces in his hands. I recall his making a comment of a similar kind when I visited him in 1977. I asked how *On History* was going, and he replied, 'Very slowly', adding that many passages that had seemed reasonably satisfactory when he had read them to the LSE Seminar on the History of Political Thought seemed rather less satisfactory when he examined them more closely as he was preparing his book. It was characteristic of him that he should have refused to hurry or take any short cuts. When I went down to the street, I glanced up at his room. He was sitting at his desk by the window, with his glasses on again, grappling

2. A Choice and Master Spirit

anew with *On History*. And I thought: He enjoys good health, he is free from administrative burdens and teaching (except for the stimulus of the weekly History of Political Thought Seminar); what a splendid way for a thinker to spend his retirement!

As well as being an eminent thinker and scholar, Michael Oakeshott was also a literary artist, a man of letters (though I am not sure that he would have liked this term). It is sometimes said of very careful writers that they weigh every word. This is obviously a hyperbole, because weighing *every* word would be the unmistakable sign of an unbalanced mind. Nevertheless, such a phrase may aptly be used about Oakeshott. He once told a colleague of mine that he usually composed about twenty drafts of anything he published. His concern for style and literary form was undoubtedly nourished by his life-long delight in the literary works of the classical world and of modern Europe. Though very English in so many ways, he was also a very cultivated European. Ostentatious displays of learning were never his style (and his footnote references were sometimes a little casual), but this wide reading enabled him to season his works with apt literary quotations: for example, a quotation from a poem by Rimbaud (typically, this is unattributed) brilliantly illuminates his discussion of Hobbes's 'generous', or magnanimous, man (*Rationalism in Politics*, p. 290).

Yet, curiously, he was rather casual about the final, printed form of his works, which are not infrequently disfigured by misprints. When I informed him about a few misprints in *On History*, he replied: 'Alas, I have never succeeded in getting into print without them: a good proof-reader is not easy to find, and I am very bad.' But some of these misprints are so patent (e.g., 'leasurely', 'Evan' – at the beginning of an article) that one wonders if the pieces in which they occur were proof-read at all. In fact, Oakeshott was sometimes careless about names and other matters of fact. Thus he was knowledgeable about cricket, and sometimes used cricketing images and analogies: e.g., *Rationalism in Politics*, pp. 181, 194, 195. But on p. 134 of this book, he refers to Mr N.A. Swanson's views; he must have meant E.W. Swanton. And on the following page, Fender's initials are given as 'G.H.', not 'P.G.H.'.

Michael Oakeshott was also a fine writer of letters. Kenneth Minogue said recently that 'he is undoubtedly one of the great letter-writers of the century'. It may perhaps be thought that the adjective 'great' is slightly exaggerated, and indeed it would appear that the age of distinguished letter-writers has passed, with the advent of the telephone, and the widespread use of dictation (a practice certainly inimical to elegant composition). One tends to associate the phrase 'great letter-writer' with persons like Mme de Sévigné or Horace Walpole, who enjoyed much leisure, and delighted in expressing their experiences and thoughts to relatives or friends, just as titles like *Hours in a Library* evoke images of Victorian men of letters in easy circumstances, composing their works in households in which the various domestic tasks were performed by servants. And Oakeshott was undoubtedly a very busy man, engaged in administration, teaching, and writing with a view to publication. Yet it is evident that he composed his letters carefully, and his many friends will treasure letters that contain felicitous turns of phrase, that delightfully recount his recent experiences or travels or recall his early life, or that express his thoughts on some intellectual topic with clarity and in his polished, idiosyncratic style. The publication of a volume of his letters would certainly be desirable. Michael may have dictated a letter occasionally, but it was definitely not his usual practice. I doubt if he ever used a typewriter, and it is impossible to imagine him sitting in front of a word-processor, as many academics do today. He belonged to a more leisurely age, in which the writing of 'research proposals' and the almost obsessive search for research grants were unknown, in the humanities at least.

Oakeshott's letters, with their small, elegant handwriting (and with wide margins on the right side of the page as well as on the left), were very singular; their form appropriately matched the elegance of the prose, and revealed, among other things, a careful, tidy mind. I once showed a recently received letter of his to an Italian poet, who had been

2. A Choice and Master Spirit

holding forth about handwriting and character. Since he knew no English, I thought this letter would provide a good test. He was very struck by it, saying that he had never seen such a hand before. He remarked the complete absence of deviations, either horizontal or vertical, and said that the writer was a vigorous person, of very firm character, who knew exactly what he wanted to say and how to say it; he was probably in his forties. The poet was astonished when I disclosed that the writer was well over eighty.

In his review of *Rationalism in Politics*,[4] W.J.M. Mackenzie made some interesting and suggestive comments about Oakeshott as a writer. I think it is a topic that merits an extended study, and it should be undertaken by someone who combines an interest and competence in language, literature and thought. There are perhaps two main tasks: analysing the prose of a modern master of English, and analysing connections between his language and his thought, or the ways in which he contrived to express his thoughts. These tasks are, to some extent, separate, but they certainly sometimes overlap.

With regard to technique, Oakeshott's punctuation and use of brackets, for instance, could be studied with profit by any aspiring writer. He was a rather heavy punctuator, and this helped to make his sentences (which were sometimes long) readily intelligible. He wanted to make his meaning quite clear, not leave the reader to guess or (by reading a sentence twice) work out exactly what he had meant. And he used brackets frequently, so that necessary qualifications or desirable incidental remarks would not obscure the main points of a sentence, as putting them between commas may do. There is another practice, conducive to clarity, that Oakeshott did not follow: Fowler's recommendation that 'that' should be used for introducing defining clauses, and 'which' (preceded by a comma) for non-defining clauses; he usually used 'which', relying on a comma preceding it to avoid undesired ambiguity.

Again, his use of imagery was very skilful. The works of the early and middle periods, in particular, contain many metaphors and similes, of which the metaphor, in 'Political

[4] *Universities Quarterly*, Vol. 17 (1963), pp. 81-3.

Education', of men 'sail[ing] a boundless and bottomless sea', with 'neither harbour for shelter nor floor for anchorage, neither starting-place nor appointed destination', which is used to characterise or illuminate political activity, is probably the best known. And one of his favourite literary devices was antithesis (one thinks of such characteristic phrases as 'more ingenious than sound', 'an activity neither to be overrated nor despised'). Some of his vocabulary is irrelevant to his *thought* (for instance, *à merveille*, not infrequent in his early writings, is not used, I think, in the post-War period), but there were notable changes in his use of some key terms, such as 'tradition' and 'practice'. I think he became more radical, linguistically, in his later years. These innovations are, perhaps, especially marked in his last two major works, and I am inclined to think that, on the whole, they did not render his writing or his thought more intelligible or accessible. In *On Human Conduct* there are some neologisms: adjectival nouns appear, such as 'intelligibles' and 'recognisables' (in phrases like 'a world of intelligibles' and 'a world of recognisables': p. 3), and the notion of 'self-enactment' (which I do not think is explained) seems to me obscure. There are other changes that do not impair intelligibility, but which are not obviously improvements: for example, 'wished-for' instead of 'desired', and ' "a going-on" ' instead of 'a happening'. Again, he came to dislike, and not use, 'of' in such phrases as 'the idea of *virtù*'. Responding to my letter about *On History*, in which I had suggested that using 'historiography' would have been an advantage, he gave one reason for avoiding it, and then added: 'And besides, it is a noun and (as you observed) I am suspicious of nouns, preferring verbs and adjectives: "historical understanding".' 'Intelligibles' and 'recognisables' are examples of adjectives that he forced to do the work of nouns; the word 'suspicious' implies that his objection (whatever exactly it was) was intellectual rather than merely stylistic (though he probably also thought, rightly, that using verbs and verbal forms conduces to a more lively style). However, the use of nouns can be avoided only to a very limited extent; and I find it interesting that such a self-conscious literary stylist was

2. A Choice and Master Spirit 37

prepared to sacrifice some degree of elegance, and even of readability, in order to express his arguments in what seemed to him a more intellectually satisfactory way.

Oakeshott's conversation was not, as John Casey has aptly observed, self-consciously clever or witty, but his writings contain many witty turns of phrase, often expressing views about the human condition very pithily. One of his abiding interests was the *moraliste* tradition of writing. Although he never wrote specific pieces on them, his works testify to his great interest in unsystematic writers like Montaigne, Bacon, Pascal, La Rochefoucauld and Vauvenargues, who expressed their thoughts on human nature and conduct, and on the human condition, not in formal philosophical treatises (though Bacon, of course, *also* wrote such works), but in essays, *pensées* and maxims, often in memorable aphorisms. And, in his unpublished Notebooks, Oakeshott himself wrote in these *genres*. In the mid-1970s, I tried to start a course on the European moralists in the European Studies Department at Lancaster University, and Michael wrote two or three times, encouraging my efforts, and saying in one letter that 'this really is the most fascinating *genre* of writing'. He may have meant that he found it more interesting than any other *genre*; or perhaps he just meant that he found it deeply interesting. Unfortunately, however, although several older colleagues said that they would love to take the course, the young men and women did not find it attractive.

Oakeshott's prose is so idiosyncratic that I always thought it would be hard to translate it into other languages. (The bibliography in his *Festschrift* lists only a German translation of *Rationalism in Politics*, which I have not seen.) My view was slightly confirmed some years ago when, in a Milan bookshop, I came across an Italian translation of Gilbert Ryle's *The Concept of Mind* (for Ryle was another fine and idiosyncratic writer). It was entitled *Lo spirito come comportamento*, and it had been recast by the translator, who provided a most interesting discussion of his reasons for making changes; but there were problems of *philosophical* style involved (he considered that Italian philosophical readers would find Ryle's prolixity with examples off-putting) as well as linguistic problems. Early in 1986, I was delighted to receive from Oakeshott a copy of the Italian translation of *On Human Conduct*, which had been published the previous year by Il Mulino, of Bologna, an excellent publisher. I perused the Preface and the pages on religion towards the end of Chapter One (one of the literary highlights of the book and, therefore, I felt, probably especially difficult to translate). I found only one mistake in these pages, and thought that Guido Maggioni had succeeded splendidly in turning Oakeshott's prose into Italian. And I now see no reason why *Rationalism in Politics* and *Hobbes on Civil Association* should not be translated into languages such as Italian (*Leviathan* has always been widely studied in Italy, though usually in translation) and French.

Oakeshott's many admirers wished that he had been a more prolific writer, but it was undoubtedly his desire to publish work that expressed his views exactly, and in a polished style, that accounts for the relatively small quantity of his publications. In these times, when academics are (or feel) under increasing pressure to publish, and sometimes yield to the temptation to publish work that is not as good as they could make it, his works provide a model that should be imitated. He wrote when he thought he had something important to say, and he worked at it until he was satisfied with the results. One tends to think of his work (as one does of that of thinkers and stylish writers like Ryle and Wittgenstein) in terms of quality rather than quantity. Oakeshott was the enemy of anything half-baked, whether in thought or style, and was hostile to talk about 'the need to increase productivity' and other current notions that are offensive to learned ears, and alien to sound scholarship. They are corrupting, because they devalue the currency of academic life: what would have been useful articles are inflated into unnecessary books, and promotion committees count the number of pages published instead of concerning themselves with their value. And knowing that Oakeshott would be reading one's work provided for many of us an additional spur to trying to make it as finished as possible.

2. A Choice and Master Spirit

Experience and its Modes has enjoyed a marked revival, following the publication of *Rationalism in Politics* in 1962. One essay in the latter volume is somewhat dated, belonging rather obviously to the early post-War period, but others (such as 'Rationalism in Politics', 'Rational Conduct', 'Political Education' and 'The Voice of Poetry in the Conversation of Mankind') will probably continue to be regarded as classic studies of intellectual history or pieces of philosophical reflection; and all the pieces in it are a delight to read, revealing Oakeshott at the top of his literary form. The later works, *On Human Conduct* and *On History*, being much more abstract in character, are more demanding (to be read at a table, with paper and pencil at hand, rather than in an armchair), though there are some delightful passages in both books (for example, the pages on religion in the former, and the story about 'The Tower of Babel' in the latter – a theme that had a constant fascination for him), which show that he had lost none of his literary skill with the passing years. *On Human Conduct*, a work of particular interest to students of political philosophy, is perhaps likely to be regarded as his masterpiece. And his writings on the philosophical problems of historical writing seem certain to retain their value for the thinkers and scholars, all too few (and few of these are historians), who are interested in these topics. Oakeshott's work on Hobbes was very influential, especially in the two decades after the War, when not many scholars were writing on Hobbes; but, despite his typically modest disclaimer in the preface to his collected pieces, *Hobbes on Civil Association* (1975), anyone who wants to study seriously the work of the great English philosopher will, I think, need to take account of Oakeshott's contribution.

Although Oakeshott was a specialist on some subjects (such as Hobbes), in general his learning was characterised by its breadth. He was familiar with all the major works of European thought and literature, and with the more important commentaries. He may not have read all the monographs on thinkers other than Hobbes (that would hardly have been possible, given his wide interests), but with regard to any topic (however esoteric it might be) in the fields of philosophy, political thought, history and literature, one could never assume that he would not know anything about it. Indeed, one had the impression that he had read everything that mattered, and that any political writer or philosopher with whose works he was not familiar was unlikely to be significant. Furthermore, he was always reflecting on what he had read (as well as on what he observed and experienced). He was not only very knowledgeable; he was a wise man. And he was able to bring his wide and varied knowledge to bear on any topic that he treated. The reflectiveness, incisiveness and wide learning of his works are very refreshing, and in these respects, too (as well as in their careful and polished style), they are a model for aspiring scholars today. Oakeshott's works are those of a highly civilised man. 'Civilisation' is a word that he used frequently; he had a strong sense of what constitutes 'our civilisation' (as he often called it), that is, European civilisation, and he thought that, for an educated man, it is an inheritance to be enjoyed.

Oakeshott was, in some ways, a rather complex man, and his reactions to things were sometimes unexpected. His works, too, are complex and various in character, and not very easy to classify. But he was a scholar, a thinker and a fine writer, and I think that he was moved by three leading impulses: the search for knowledge, the search for truth, and devotion to beauty (or what he called 'poetry').

The first two obviously go well together; indeed, any sharp distinction between them is impossible (for 'knowledge' implies 'true' or 'genuine' knowledge). Nevertheless, there is an important difference between the approach of the scholar, learned man or *savant*, who takes an area (or areas) of knowledge for his 'province' (an approach exemplified by historians such as Namier and Elton, or literary historians such as Sainte-Beuve and Saintsbury), and the approach typical of philosophers, in which a dominant concern is the 'quality' of knowledge, possible or attained; they distinguish between various kinds of knowledge, and examine criteria and theories of truth.

An unusual feature of Oakeshott's works is that both these impulses are conspicuous; sometimes they are developed separately, but more often they are found together. Thus, he said of his essay 'Rational Conduct' that it was 'both philosophical and historical' in character. Again, *On Human Conduct* manifests interest in both the ideal and the actual character of the modern European state.

Oakeshott's endless curiosity about human activity and thought found full scope in his study of philosophy, political thought and history (especially, though certainly not only, intellectual history). And his reading of 'literary' works, such as novels and poetry, satisfied his interest in the diversity of human conduct, motives and intentions, and appealed to his pronounced sense of beauty.

Oakeshott's concern for truth is evidenced by his philosophical works, especially by *Experience and its Modes, On Human Conduct* and *On History*, in which he explored such broad themes as various modes of human experience, the character and divisions of knowledge, the nature of civil association and of the modern state, and the nature of historical knowledge and writing. In the last two books, achieving coherence and the exact expression of his views became almost a noble obsession, pursued tirelessly, even relentlessly.

Oakeshott did not pass the years of retirement in making a book out of his lectures on the history of political thought, or devoting himself to certain areas of intellectual history (as Ernest Barker, another polymath, had largely done, during his very productive retirement). Instead, during the last period of his life, the 'voice' of the philosopher (not of the scholar or intellectual historian) became dominant again, as it had in early manhood, in his first book, though the philosophical and literary styles were markedly different. As I suggested earlier, the writing of fine prose, a life-long concern, to some extent became subordinated to the search for, and lucid expression of, philosophical truth, especially truths about the character of the modern state and of historical writing.

Michael Oakeshott will be remembered with affection and gratitude by all who were fortunate enough to know him, for his personal qualities, his generosity, kindness, straightforwardness, integrity, good humour and gaiety, as well as for his striking intellectual qualities, which are manifested and preserved in his published works. He was a remarkable man, one of the 'choice and master spirits of this age'.

3

Modes and Modesty

Kenneth Minogue

Michael Oakeshott was above all an educated man, as he himself understood education: someone who had been immersed in the cultural traditions of a human world, and who refracted these traditions through a self-conscious and cultivated individuality. He loved novels, poetry, history, argument, conversation and much else. Out of conversation he was to construct a famous image in order to explain a complex philosophical idea. He made his life within the university, which he distinguished from 'the world', but he was very far from being an impractical and absent-minded scholar. Orderly in domestic arrangements, he was also a skilled handy man (he knocked together two cottages in a stone quarry in Dorset as his last habitation) and a highly efficient administrator of the Government Department at the London School of Economics from 1951 till his retirement in 1969. When the dogs of war were unleashed in 1939, he went into the army, impelled by an unostentatious patriotism. There too he amply proved his capabilities.

Oakeshott's reputation in the wider world did not always correspond to his actual character. Philosophers no less than poets construct personae with which they express certain sorts of positions. Hostile readers of the essay 'Rationalism in Politics' saw the rationalist compared to a foreigner, or a man out of his social class – 'a butler or an observant housemaid has the advantage of him' – and conjured up a patrician contemptuous of his inferiors. He was nothing of the sort, but romantic, considerate to all he came in contact with, and intellectually fastidious. His individuality was obvious not only in the style of his writing, but in the elegance of his handwriting; he is undoubtedly one of the great letter-writers of the century. He was generous in these outpourings to his friends, and his conception of friendship was essentially modern: friends were those you delighted in. Affable and approachable, he was the last person of whom one would be inclined to say that he did not suffer fools gladly. His actual judgments, however, were sharp and precise.

Oakeshott's first book, *Experience and its Modes*, appeared in 1933. It was a self-confident performance, and its virtues were both literary and philosophical. It fell, however, dead-born from the press, and a small issue had not even been sold out when war came. Susan Stebbing said it was all in Bradley, but Collingwood approved particularly of its treatment of history. What it certainly did was to provide Oakeshott with plenty to think about. One might almost say that it laid down a research programme, except for the fact that Oakeshott detested jargon. He usually had a sound grip on the technicalities of whatever he dealt with – this grasp occasionally surfacing in a savage aside – but he understood philosophy always to transcend abstractions. Strictly averse to academic pretentiousness, he disliked unnecessary parades of learning. He aimed to be both professional and accessible.

Experience and its Modes, however, presented a view of philosophy immensely at odds with all contemporary opinion. In terms of the later image of the conversation of mankind, philosophy commented on the 'voices' in the conversation but made no direct utterance in it:

> The voice of philosophy ... is unusually conversable. There is no body of philosophical 'knowledge' to become detached from the activity of philosophising: hence Hume's perception of the supremely civilising quality of philosophical reflection, and hence the difficulty which both men of science and of business have in understanding what philosophy is about

3. Modes and Modesty

and their frequent attempts to transform it into something more familiar to themselves.[1]

Philosophy is the transcendence of what is abstract in the modes; it is the attempt to understand experience in its full concreteness by way of inquiry into the postulates of human activity. This is at once a very grand conception of philosophy, in the Continental rather than the British manner, but it is combined with an unyielding insistence that philosophy can never replace, correct or even improve what is done with the modes.[2] The icy clarity of those cloud-capped peaks would melt if dragged down to the lower slopes. Generations of students, yearning to be assured that everything was useful, laboured in vain to induce him to admit that the reading of Kant's moral theory, for example, entailed changes in actual moral conduct. It might, he insisted, or it might not, but it was certainly a contingent matter. As he remarked on the last page of *Experience and its Modes*:

> There is perhaps something decadent, something even depraved, in an attempt to achieve a completely coherent world of experience; for such a pursuit requires us to renounce for the time being everything which can be called good or evil, everything which can be valued or rejected as valueless. And no matter how far we go with it, we shall not easily forget the sweet delight which lies in the empty kisses of abstraction.

Like Hegel, then, Oakeshott takes human beings to live amidst abstraction, and the modes are the spectacles which abstract from the concrete whole of experience and thus enable us to respond to some manageable aspect of reality – science, history, art, and above all, practice. Practice is recognised as having a dangerous centrality. It is agents engaged in the *dance macabre* of human appetite. It is so much the most primitive and general of all forms of

---

[1] *Rationalism in Politics* (1962), p. 205. A second edition of this work, with additional essays, was published by Liberty Press in 1991.
[2] This point is neatly expounded on pp. 27-31 of *On Human Conduct* (1975), where Oakeshott concludes some epistemological reflections by discussing Plato's allegory of the cave.

experience that 'it is not the prevalence of this belief which should surprise us, but the fact that it is not universal'.[3] In fact it very nearly is universal, even in cultivated circles, even though many people who hold it do not actually act in terms of it.

Oakeshott found the error, as he saw it, of seeing everything in practical terms especially obnoxious, whatever form it might take: pragmatism, utilitarianism or ideologies such as Marxism. It was for him precisely the triumph of civilisation to have facilitated the emergence of other modes in which to explore and enjoy the world. In *Experience and its Modes* he specified science and history as other modes, but he noted that there was no necessary limit to their number. Later, in 'The Voice of Poetry in the Conversation of Mankind',[4] he explored art. Throughout this concern with modes, he sought to clarify what he took to be the most insidious of intellectual errors – *ignoratio elenchi*, irrelevance, or slipping from one mode into another. Water, to use an obvious example, has little in common with H_2O, and neither has much relation to the poetic images of water in *The Ancient Mariner*. Each mode plays by its own rules, as it were, and to mix them is like playing basketball in the middle of a game of football. This mistake was remarkably prevalent in the social sciences (which in his more fastidious moments he would regard as a misnomer). The idea, for example, that history can be turned into data for scientific generalisation is a piece of intellectual butchery. A project like historical sociology, treating of revolutions, for example, will lose the specificity of history without gaining the universality of science. Above all, as we shall see, the belief that the state can be improved in terms of some philosophical argument is the logical mistake of thinking that a concept *entails* a practical conclusion. Those who imagine that a work of art can tell them truths about the world will arrive at some pretty rum conclusions.

If he did not quite believe, like A.N. Prior, that philosophy was a conceptual service industry, akin to mowing the lawn

---

[3] *Experience and its Modes* (1933), p. 247.
[4] Reprinted in *Rationalism in Politics*.

3. Modes and Modesty

or paring fingernails, he was in no doubt that any civilisation in which the conversation lacked philosophical awareness was highly vulnerable to confusion. The muddle of modern political discussion especially concerned him, in particular such confusions as that between the desirability of a proposal and its authority, comparisons which threatened a constitutional way of doing things on which freedom depended. It was dismay at this drift towards despotism which explains the polemical tone of post-war writings when Oakeshott was editing the *Cambridge Journal*. His fear, as he later expressed it, was that:

> In recent controversies, the conversation, both in public and within ourselves, has become boring because it has been expressed by two voices, the voice of practical activity and the voice of 'science': to know and to contrive are our pre-eminent occupations ... for a conversation to be appropriated by one or two voices is an insidious vice because in the passage of time it takes on the appearance of a virtue ... An excluded voice ... may gain a hearing by imitating the voices of the monopolists; but it will be a hearing only for a counterfeit utterance.[5]

Few things make that last sentence more plausible than the typical reception of Oakeshott's own writings, including some very distinguished misinterpreters.[6]

Before turning to his view of politics, we may clarify his philosophical intentions in terms of one mode in which he took a particular interest: history. It was where he started from, and in seminars for students at LSE in the seventies, he was still working to get clear precisely what characterised it. What always interested him were the epistemological minima by which a mode might be understood. One unreflective view about history is that it tells us what happened in the past, but such a view sets up impossible truth conditions for the historian. Where can he find the actual past by which to check the account which he

---

[5] 'The Voice of Poetry in the Conversation of Mankind' in *Rationalism in Politics*, p. 202.

[6] For rip-roaring incomprehension, it is hard to beat the essays collected in *Political Theory* 4 (August 1976). The exception is that by Lee Auspitz. The issue also contains an irritated rejoinder by Oakeshott himself.

has composed out of a variety of evidences?

Indeed it is precisely the postulation of a past which makes history 'modal', an 'arrest' of experience. Experience can only ever be present, but history must constitute itself in terms of the abstract idea of a past. Further, history has no monopoly of this idea, and a central part in Oakeshott's philosophy is played by the insistence that it is a serious mistake to believe that any utterance referring to the past is historical. Confronted by a production such as *The History of the Communist Party of the Soviet Union (Bolsheviks)* which was rewritten with every swerve of the Bolshevik regime, Oakeshott took the view that this was not at all bad history, but political practice, no doubt appropriate for its own purposes. Many transactions of practical life – from property rights to sustaining individual and corporate identities – require what he called 'a practical past'. Getting its history wrong, Renan once remarked, is an essential part of nationalism, but Oakeshott would have commented that nationalists are not concerned with history at all. Attempting to correct the 'history' in such accounts of the past was the basic error of irrelevance – a category mistake, as a later jargon came to describe it. Wherever such practical pasts appear, of course, they strongly qualify the very possibility of actual historical inquiry: we already know all too fatally well what we purport to be investigating. This was one reason why he thought that contemporary history, whatever intellectual merits it might have, could not be properly historical.

In making this point, he could not resist one of those jokes by with which he often succeeded in offending the humourless:

> This 'historian' adores the past; but the world today has perhaps less place for those who love the past then ever before ... For it wishes only to learn from the past and it constructs a 'living past' which repeats with spurious authority the utterances put into its mouth. But to the 'historian' this is a piece of obscene necromancy: the past he adores is dead. The world has neither love nor respect for what is dead, wishing only to recall it to life again. It deals with the past as with a man, expecting it to talk sense and

3. Modes and Modesty

have something to say apposite to its plebeian 'causes' and engagements. But for the 'historian', for whom the past is dead and irreproachable, the past is feminine. He loves it as a mistress of whom he never tires and whom he never expects to talk sense.[7]

What this passage reveals most of all is Oakeshott's view of a university. It is a place having its own very specific academic excitement, the passion to learn, understand and explain. This delicate passion, which has so long been sustained by the institutional remoteness of universities, is vulnerable to the blatant excitements and deafening causes of the practical world. Scholarship is not everyone's cup of tea, and the fatal success of technology in modern times has given universities a vogue which bids fair to destroy them, as they are engulfed by wave after wave of the shock troops of practicality.

Education was the central business of Oakeshott's life, and he conceived of it as the cultivation of a disposition to understand rules and meanings of many kinds. It required conversational manners, a certain deference towards the learned, and a humility in relation to one's cultural inheritance. It was a disposition as likely to be found in a thoughtful gardener or reflective carpenter as in some bright and overconfident undergraduate. The philosopher John Searle, in a not unsympathetic review of some essays on education[8] complained that Oakeshott's educated person 'does not look as if he would produce any intellectual revolutions, or even upset very many intellectual apple carts'. Leaving aside the question of whether Searle or Oakeshott would come out best on the apple-cart test, we may observe that it is a serious mistake to expect that *education* would *produce* any specific human type. It is not a production process. What it might be expected to do is protect the educated against the supremely vulgar error of mistaking current enthusiasms for absolute truth.

---

[7] 'The Activity of being an Historian', reprinted in *Rationalism in Politics*, p. 166ff.

[8] Michael Oakeshott, *The Voice of Liberal Learning*, edited by Timothy Fuller, 1989. Searle's review appeared in the *New York Review of Books*, Dec. 6, 1990.

Oakeshott sometimes uses the metaphor of current, or flow, in describing a tradition of education, and his attitude is charmingly captured in the words he used in a talk to students at Colorado College in 1974:

> I have crossed half the world to find myself in familiar surroundings: a place of learning. The occasion is a cheerful one: the celebration of the centenary of your foundation, and I hope you will not think me patronising if I first express my admiration for you and all others who, through the centuries, sailing under the flag of the Liberal Arts, have, with becoming humility, summoned succeeding generations to the enjoyment of their human inheritance. But it is an occasion also for reflection ... This is a large order, and you will forgive me if I respond to it only in part. Education is a transaction between teachers and learners, but I shall be concerned only with learners, with what there is to be learned and (in the first place) with learning as the distinguishing mark of a human being. A man is what he learns to become: this is the human condition.

That this view is not easy to commend in modern circumstances is clear from the fact that Searle goes on to argue that liberal education today is in a bad way because it lacks – a theory. He proceeds to sketch out such a thing in the form of a schedule of intellectual desirabilities for the modern citizen: a bit of Plato, some Marx, recognition for the culture of minorities, relativity and a bit of quantum theory, some literature and sundry other fragments to be shored against our ruin. Compare this with the words Oakeshott admiringly quotes from William Cory, a famous Eton schoolmaster:

> At school 'you are not engaged so much in acquiring knowledge as in making mental efforts under criticism. ... A certain amount of knowledge you can indeed with average faculties acquire so as to retain; nor need you regret the hours you spend on much that is forgotten, for the shadow of lost knowledge at least protects you from many illusions. But you go to a great school not so much for knowledge as for arts and habits; for the habit of attention, for the art of expression, for the art of assuming at a moment's notice, a

3. Modes and Modesty

new intellectual position, for the art of entering quickly into another person's thoughts, for the habit of submitting to censure and refutation, for the art of indicating assent or dissent in graduated terms, for the habit of regarding minute points of accuracy, for the art of working out what is possible in a given time, for taste, discrimination, for mental courage and mental soberness. And above all you go to a great school for self-knowledge.'[9]

It may seem that I have taken the long way round in arriving at the political philosophy which is Oakeshott's main claim on our attention. But this is merely to follow Oakeshott's own practice of situating any subject in a wider context. Politics, being a human activity, require an understanding of human activity itself. In reading Hobbes, he looked to what Hobbes believed to be 'the local and transitory mischief in which the universal predicament of mankind' appeared. Oakeshott was in no doubt that his own time exhibited such a local, if perhaps not transitory, mischief, and the thread to follow in eliciting his thoughts on this subject is his deep preoccupation with the myth of the Tower of Babel along with its analogues in other traditions. The myth expresses the human propensity 'to seek perfection as the crow flies'. The modern world appears in these terms as a Promethean succession of Titans ambitious to turn men into gods and to transcend the human condition. The original Titans were repelled, according to Plato, because they did not understand nature, something which their scientific successors, from Bacon on, have sought to remedy. The punishment for the builders of the Tower of Babel was to be plunged into a confusion of tongues. Oakeshott believed that the political discourse of modern Europeans had fallen into a similar confusion, and much of his intellectual concern was to restore some clarity to it. But we must first consider the Babelian project from which the confusion stemmed.

Oakeshott called it 'rationalism'. Rationalism was a general form of human activity, now also dominant in politics, which promised qualitative improvements in

---

[9] Quoted in 'The Voice of Poetry in the Conversation of Mankind', *Rationalism in Politics*, p. 200.

human life from the application of abstract ideas. Oakeshott defined politics as 'the activity of attending to the general arrangements of a set of people whom chance or choice have brought together'.[10] The rationalist believed that there was a perfect and final way of arranging people. Rights, Justice, Racial Purity, Community and many other such terms stood for bodies of doctrine prescribing a better world. They were forms of snake oil capable of being taken by an unsophisticated populace as elixirs of perpetual political health. Such rationalist politics respond to the needs of the politically inexperienced, and invariably require a Platonic accession to power of exponents of the particular knowledge in question – revolutionaries, experts, commissars etc.

What seemed intellectually most significant about rationalism was its doctrine of knowledge, and Oakeshott diagnosed its weakness by distinguishing between technical and practical knowledge. Technique can be made explicit and formalised, but whoever seeks to 'apply' it unavoidably calls upon a kind of practical knowledge – in fact a set of sensibilities, dispositions, aptnesses, recognitions, judgments etc. – which cannot be taught by formula. Mistaking the part of knowledge for the whole, the rationalist imagines that his projects follow logically from his doctrines. Since logic could never in fact supply the connection, the rationalist has merely mistaken his own dogmatic convictions for reality. The result was that modern European politics had fallen into the hands of crazed sorcerer's apprentices who imagined they could effect a once-and-for-all transformation of human life. No doubt an Attlee with his Fabian doctrine to hand was infinitely preferable to Adolf Hitler purporting to read his actions off from a doctrine of racial purity, but from this elevated point of view, both were rationalists – incompetent cooks, if one may adapt one of Oakeshott's favourite metaphors, trying to pass off hamburger as rump steak.

Ideology of this kind, he argued in 'Political Education', purported to be a bright new politics-transforming idea, but could at best be nothing more than a 'crib' whose only value

[10] Ibid., p. 112.

3. Modes and Modesty

would be the traces of some actual political tradition from which it had been abridged. Some such 'cribs' were in even worse state: they were not even derived from a political tradition, but intellectualisations of some other human activity, such as warfare or economic production. Twentieth-century politics had become so corrupt that statesmen felt naked unless they could boast a doctrine, yet the truth about political activity was that it could never be anything else but 'the pursuit of intimations'. This phrase became a battleground between Oakeshott and a horde of vengeful rationalists who thought it merely a fancy way of saying that governments ought never to do anything at all.

We may indeed take the doctrine that politics can be nothing but the pursuit of intimations as a good example of the misunderstandings and incomprehensions which frequently arose between Oakeshott and his fellow practitioners of the study of politics. We may elucidate it as involving two theses. The first is that the political world is a complex of circumstances within which we only find our direction by responding to the current movement of things. The controversy over whether a bowler in cricket should be permitted by the rules to throw the ball (to use his own example) was argued out not in terms of the essence of cricket (from which nothing practical follows) but from looking at how bowling had evolved. Another of his examples was the enfranchisement of women, which responded to an incoherence in the position of women resulting from a great variety of social changes – in technology, in taste, in moral attitudes, etc. To argue this issue in terms of the timeless rights of women merely adds anachronism to the irrelevance of abstraction. Natural law beliefs had been around for a very long time before they found application to the franchise of women in a liberal democracy. The second thesis involved in the doctrine of the pursuit of intimations is that no practical proposal necessarily follows from any abstract commitment. 'Peace' can lead you straight into war, and often has. This thesis might well be restated, then, as a challenge to those who reject it: Expound in detail the steps which *necessarily* lead from an abstract commitment to the details of a piece of legislation. The recent vogue in the philosophy of science for treating facts as sustained by a whole nest of theoretical assumptions may make this doctrine less opaque than it seemed in the middle years of the century.

To say that all hell broke loose over this phrase would be an exaggeration; far more a storm in a teacup. What certainly happened was a procession of political theorists unmasking it as a covert attempt to stop radical reform in its tracks. There are still extant textbooks which absurdly report the doctrine as being that politics *ought to be* the pursuit of intimations. It was invariably attacked as being a recommendation. Much of this comedy derived from another of those irrelevances Oakeshott attacked: since he had been identified as a conservative, any general doctrine he advanced must be doctrinaire. It is not merely that this particular inference fails, but the identification itself requires clarification. Oakeshott has indeed given a sympathetic account of what a conservative disposition might be, and he has presented compelling reasons for thinking that governments which use the power of a civil association to impose upon their subjects some projects or enterprise recommended on abstract moral grounds are engaging in an activity different from what may properly be recognised as politics. As he remarks in 'The Tower of Babel':

> The pursuit of perfection as the crow flies ... is an activity ... suitable for individuals, but not for societies ... For a society ... the penalty is a chaos of conflicting ideals, the disruption of a common life, and the reward is the renown which attaches to monumental folly. Or, to interpret the myth in a more light-hearted fashion: human life is a gamble; but while the individual must be allowed to bet according to his inclinations (on the favourite or on an outsider), society should always back the field.[11]

Since a great deal of modern politics has been an attempt to build a new Tower of Babel, Oakeshott has not been short of targets on which to exercise his scorn. But in terms of actual

---

[11] 'The Tower of Babel', ibid., p. 59ff.

3. Modes and Modesty

politics, there are very few if any policies which his writings would rule out on principle.

This becomes quite apparent if we turn to the three essays which make up his most sustained treatment of the fundamental problems of politics, *On Human Conduct* (1975). Typically, he began with the vaster question of what it was to theorise human conduct, and especially with the question (fundamental in the philosophy of history) of how contingent relationships may be understood without turning them into something else. The schematic structure of *Experience and its Modes* is relaxed in favour of a more pluralistic epistemology composed of a variety of different 'conditional platforms of understanding'. Such a scheme allows Oakeshott to move in the second essay to consider politics and the state. But these are not the words we encounter. 'Politics' is cast to one side as a term so indiscriminately used as to be better avoided. 'The state' is a modern historical entity, which he treats in the discursive third essay. What he actually talks about is 'civil association', understood as an ideal condition in terms of its postulates.

Civil association is not an easy thing to grasp. The most characteristic activity of human beings is banding together in order to achieve some satisfactory outcome, perhaps temporary as in a dinner party, or continuously, as with a church or a union. These familiar forms of association are here called 'enterprise associations'. But political philosophers, especially the best of them (Oakeshott singles out Aristotle, Hobbes and Hegel particularly) have always been aware that the *polis* or the *civitas* was not an association of this kind. Just as practice is so dominant a mode as to absorb all else, so associations for some specific purpose are so familiar that it is difficult to exhibit a kind of association which, in not arising from the projects of its members, leaves them free to pursue their own purposes. The model for such an association might be found in the set of people who speak a language. Such people are associated together only in their subjection to the rules and vocabulary of the language. What they actually utter in the language is up to them. Civil association along these lines is *cives* linked only by their subjection to a common set of rules. Oakeshott takes it that Aristotle meant something of this kind by *autarkeia* (self-sufficiency).[12] This distinction leads on to a theory of the rule of law in terms of non-instrumental rules. The advantage of bringing this machinery to bear upon the modern state is that it outflanks the distinction between the individual and the state, often fatally construed as a zero-sum distribution of rights. This is a promising but underdeveloped area of Oakeshott's thought, so much so that Paul Franco, in presenting an excellent full-length account of Oakeshott's political philosophy,[13] has recourse to some writings of Shirley Letwin in order to elucidate it.

Oakeshott was a sceptic, and a bit of a dandy, and his personality and his doctrines were linked in various ways. Starting, as Noel O'Sullivan pointed out in an obituary, from a very strong sense of the conditionalities of thought and the insecurities of human existence, he found the human world a marvellous creation. Loving it as he did, and blessed with a happy temperament, he saw no need to entrench his tastes and admirations in creaky intellectual commitments such as natural law, philosophy, progress or the other recourses and happy endings which mankind has invented for itself. If something were needed to meet this need, it ought to be a religion; but such an intrusion into academic life was merely one more of those irrelevances plaguing mankind. Religion he construed in a Christian idiom as 'a reconciliation to the unavoidable dissonances of the human condition ... a graceful response'[14] and he was thus deeply intolerant of the inverted religiosity of ideologies which fed political ambition by preaching misery and discontent.

Oakeshott's work will survive time's decay because it is original, profound and pugnacious. In dealing with abstract issues such as law and civil association, he unravels many a tangled thread. In the final essay of *On Human Conduct*, his reflections on the experience of modern European politics leave no cliché undisturbed. The tradition has been

---

[12] *On Human Conduct*, p. 110. The reference is to Book VII of the *Politics*.
[13] *The Political Philosophy of Michael Oakeshott* (Yale University Press, 1990).
[14] *On Human Conduct*, p. 81.

thought through anew in all its aspects, and the understanding is animated by a frank disdain for the infatuation with servility which is often barely concealed in much modern theory and practice. Oakeshott may not have saved us from rationalism, but he has left us with no excuse for ignorance of its ravages.

4

Philosopher of Practice

John Casey

When Michael Oakeshott died just before Christmas 1990, in his nineteenth year, he was awarded the rare tribute of a *Times* leader. In this he was described as 'nothing less than the chief reanimator of conservatism after the long dominance of socialism over political theory in twentieth-century Britain'.

Oakeshott was indeed a great philosopher of conservatism. More important, he was perhaps the greatest British political philosopher since John Stuart Mill – perhaps since Burke. Yet he was, paradoxically, famous in his lifetime without being at all well-known. He was revered by his disciples, of course. But outside that happy band (for 'Oakeshottians' are the most genial collection of disciples one is likely to come across; compare them with 'Leavisites') he was not very influential. At any rate he was never fashionable. Oakeshott's work has not become part of the common currency of debate in the academy, unlike the writings of (for instance) Rawls, Nozick, Dworkin or Rorty. There is a remarkable disparity between the claims made for Oakeshott by his admirers during his lifetime, and, still more strikingly, after his death in several very full and serious obituaries, and his comparative neglect by many scholars in his fields.

Indeed many who were not convinced – or entranced – by Oakeshott simply ignored or dismissed him. Others regarded him as essentially a sceptic with a gift for sinuous

4. Philosopher of Practice

eloquence of expression, but no solid doctrine. We can certainly not be confident that he is widely understood.

Oakeshott was an immensely popular lecturer at Cambridge before moving first to Nuffield College in 1949, and then to LSE in 1951. Those who remember his lectures say that they had the impression of a measured, elegant mind. The argument was leisurely, indeed sinuous, insinuating.

It is said of a great teacher sufficiently often to have become a cliché that you would have had to have sat at his feet to get the true flavour of the *man*. And it is true that those who were converted by Oakeshott were usually captivated; that they yielded to a manner as much as to a doctrine. But T.S. Eliot wrote that 'genuine poetry can communicate before it is understood'. Oakeshott's manner and prose were related to something which anyone would be prepared to call 'doctrine' who was not wedded to that procrustean view of knowledge that he called, famously, 'rationalism'.

Of course he did have a doctrine – about practical knowledge. This underpins the importance that – like virtually all conservative thinkers – he attaches to the idea of tradition.

A notion of tradition is an indispensable part of Oakeshott's thought. It is indispensable, not in the sense that he has a sentimental regard for it, or that he is a *laudator temporis acti*, finding philosophical reasons for what Young Fogeys believe on instinct, but because he argues that political understanding and political education would be strictly unintelligible without it.

It was Oakeshott's best-known doctrine that to approach politics on the basis of a prior ideology, or to treat it simply as a means to some ends which can be identified independently of existing traditions of political practice, deforms our political understanding. He expressed the idea in a famous passage about political activity being like sailing a boundless and bottomless sea. It could not be further from the world-view of the Conservative party during the past fifteen years. In spirit it is closer to T.S. Eliot in *The Dry Salvages* ('Fare forward, travellers! not escaping from the past/Into different lives, or into any future ...') rather than to any thinker who may offer programmes to politicians.

Oakeshott himself conceded that this would be found by some 'a depressing doctrine'. It is certainly one which has called forth vehement dissent. To many, the idea that all we have to go by in politics is tradition, and the limited possibilities of innovation that traditional practices intimate, is a strategy for ruling out *a priori* every sort of radicalism.

Yet Oakeshott's fundamental doctrine is not about tradition but about practical knowledge and practical wisdom. Philosophers commonly distinguish between 'knowing that' and 'knowing how'. I know John Major is Prime Minister. But I also have practical knowledge. I can ride a bicycle, play the piano, speak English. Some practical knowledge can be formulated in rules, principles, maxims. It can be learned from books – legal textbooks, cookery books, computer manuals.

Not all practical knowledge can be summed up in rules. We think that learning to play a musical instrument will require a talented teacher. The great physician will have the factual and scientific knowledge necessary to his work, but beyond that he will have a gift, an insight, an art which cannot be formulated as a set of technical rules, and which is passed on through personal influence.

Standing behind Oakeshott's thought there is Aristotle's doctrine of *phronêsis* – practical wisdom. Aristotle spoke of the *phronimos* – the man of practical wisdom – who can deliberate not just about specific goods, as the stockbroker deliberates about investments, or the physician about health, but about 'what sorts of thing conduce to the good life in general'. And Aristotle suggests that if we want to know what sorts of thing conduce to the good life in general, we will be guided by what the *phronimos* would choose. For Aristotle the wisdom of the *phronimos* can be seen as a model for political activity: 'Political and practical wisdom are the same state of mind, but their essence is not the same.'

Oakeshott's celebrated lecture 'Political Education' shows

4. Philosopher of Practice

the signs of this Aristotelian inheritance. Oakeshott succeeded Harold Laski as Professor of Politics at LSE, and this was his inaugural lecture. With exquisite courtesy – which yet could not have diminished the anguish felt by many of his listeners – he introduced his audience to a style of political thought as far removed as possible from the socialism of Laski.

In the lecture Oakeshott defined politics as 'the activity of attending to the general arrangements of a set of people whom chance or choice have brought together', and particularly of 'hereditary, co-operative groups, many of them of ancient lineage ... which we call "states"'. For Oakeshott, this 'attending to' arrangements is something quite different from inventing arrangements, or from founding one's politics upon some abstract theory such as democracy, or the rights of man, or scientific materialism, or the free market. There cannot be political understanding or beliefs outside an actual political tradition, any more than there could be a scientific theory in the absence of a tradition of science, or cookery books without an actual practice of cuisine. Ideas such as democracy, or the rights of man cannot be the foundation of politics, because they make sense only as abbreviations of actual practices and traditions.

This does not mean that we cannot reasonably use such terms at all. When English statesmen (for instance) have talked of freedom, they have not been invoking a purely abstract idea, but have been appealing to specific traditions, which are enshrined in English history and in the common law tradition. Even the American Founding Fathers, in formulating their Bill of Rights, were unconsciously guided by what was intimated by the habits of behaviour which they had inherited from the English political tradition.

It is thus that Oakeshott arrives at his celebrated opposition to 'rationalism in politics'. The rationalist is mistaken about the nature of politics because he does not see it as the application of *phronêsis*. He is inclined to think of politics as the means to some desirable end – developing the resources of the country or establishing the Kingdom of Christ upon earth. A notable statement of the rationalist position was Lenin's: 'The Soviets plus electricity equals Communism.'

Oakeshott wrote approvingly about Keats's idea of Negative Capability – that condition in which 'man is capable of being in uncertainties, mysteries, doubts, without any irritable reaching after fact and reason'. He quoted Keats in his essay 'The Universities' – which seems to me one of the finest things he wrote. He connects a university education with Negative Capability:

> The great and characteristic gift of a university was first that of an interval. Here was an opportunity to put aside the hot allegiances of youth without the necessity of acquiring new loyalties to take their place. Here was an interval in which a man might refuse to commit himself. Here was a break in the tyrannical course of irreparable events; a period in which to look round upon the world without the sense of an enemy at one's back or the insistent pressure to make up one's mind; a moment in which one was relieved of the necessity of 'coming to terms with oneself' or of entering the fierce partisan struggle of the world outside.[1]

Here he was relating university education to 'the good life in general'. And he showed himself quite untouched by less humane, more restrictive, visions of education.

It is certainly true that to give a bald outline of some of Michael Oakeshott's better-known theories in political philosophy is not to give much sense of the man. For he was a rare modern example of a thinker who lived his philosophy. He was, for instance, a brilliant conversationalist. His conversation had a curiously innocent, child-like quality, often exceedingly funny, but never self-consciously 'witty'. His talk was always that of a philosopher, but those enchanted by his company often did not realise it.

One of Oakeshott's enduring symbols of human life was what he called 'the conversation of mankind'. Conversation is what distinguished the civilised man from the barbarian. This idea was part of his metaphysics. As a philosopher in the tradition of Hegel and F.H. Bradley, he conceived of a number of 'worlds' of human discourse, with no one world

---

[1] 'The Universities', in *The Voice of Liberal Learning* (1989), p. 127.

4. Philosopher of Practice

taking precedence over the others. These are the worlds of history, of science and of practical life. The task of philosophy is to take a synoptic view of these worlds, to hold them in relation to each other, not to insist upon one at the expense of the others. It will not (for instance) declare that science alone is the 'real' world. Philosophy is not itself a form of knowledge superior to the others. Rather the relation between them is like that between voices in a properly conducted conversation.

Oakeshott used to attend meetings of a group of Tory MPs, dons and journalists. Very occasionally Mrs Thatcher also attended. At one meeting she engaged in what can only be called a wrangle with a distinguished and civilised journalist, noted for his love of elegant paradox. It was a discussion in which *one* voice was dominant. Oakeshott's sole contribution to the debate, after much apparent reflection, was to wind up and set going a cageful of mechanical singing birds.

Oakeshott never accepted any public honours. He was the opposite of an academic grandee. Indeed his self-effacement – or self-sufficiency – was legendary. Sir Peregrine Worsthorne – who became Editor of the *Sunday Telegraph* – having interrupted his undergraduate career at Cambridge to join the army during the war, found himself sharing a tent for six months with Oakeshott in Holland. He noticed with a young man's incredulity that this forty-year-old's interest in pretty Dutch girls was not less than his. He also found his fellow officer, although of no particular intellectual pretensions, an appreciative audience for his views on the philosophy of history, politics and other topics, delivered with all the confidence of one who had just won a History Scholarship to Peterhouse. It was with surprise verging upon horror that on his return to Cambridge after the war, he attended a course of lectures on European political thought to be given by the celebrated M.J. Oakeshott, and saw his old army chum mounting the rostrum. Conversely there must have been many who have opened *A Guide to the Classics*, of which Oakeshott and Guy Griffith were co-authors, only to discover that it is about how to pick a Derby winner.

I did not come to know Oakeshott until the last twenty years of his life. He was for some years a rare visitor to Cambridge. I remember vividly a first sight of him, in the Combination Room at luncheon. I knew it must be Oakeshott – just because he looked so distinguished. His face made me think of Dryden's in the portrait by Kneller. (I still think there is a resemblance.)

My own friendship with Michael got off to a rather eccentric start. As I have said, he had not been a very regular visitor to Cambridge for some while. When he was elected to a Fellowship at Nuffield College, Oxford, in 1949, he had been a college lecturer at Caius for nearly twenty years – that being the period under the Statutes which entitled one to resign one's lectureship and become a life fellow. The College Council stretched a point, and elected him into a life fellowship when it was not strictly obliged to do so. It was a mark of esteem and friendship.

As his seventieth birthday approached, some Fellows felt that he should be encouraged to come back more often and get to know some of the younger Fellows. It was decided that we should hold a dinner for his birthday, and I was deputed to arrange it. We asked a number of Fellows of Caius and friends of his from London. Only days before the dinner, I telephoned him and read him a list of those who would be coming. I asked whether there was anyone else – from London or Cambridge – who should be invited. 'Yes,' he said, 'Father Gilbey.'

So I telephoned Monsignor Alfred Gilbey and invited him to the dinner. He expressed surprise and pleasure at the 'undeserved honour' as he called it (with, I thought, unnecessary humility) and accepted the invitation.

The Monsignor arrived last and asked to be taken to Oakeshott. (His exact words were 'Take me to the birthday boy.') They met, looked sharply at each other for a moment, and embraced. I was glad to have arranged that such old friends should be seated next to each other for the whole evening. They talked with animation throughout.

It was only later that I realised what the sharp look had meant. They had never met before in their lives. I believe they never met afterwards. When Oakeshott had said

'Gilbey' he had in fact meant Father Thomas *Gilby*, the General Editor of the *Summa* of Aquinas, and a very old friend. It was characteristic of Oakeshott that he was perfectly happy to spend his seventieth birthday in the (certainly delightful) company of a complete stranger.

Oakeshott remained devoted to the College. He described himself on the title page of his second *magnum opus* – *On Human Conduct* – simply as 'Fellow of Gonville and Caius College'. This did not mean that he was not equally devoted to LSE, but that he regarded Caius (as he said in his extremely brief speech on his seventieth birthday) as 'my own place'. He regarded himself as an Augustinian Christian (although a sense of human corruption never seems to have played a part in his thought) and always attended Chapel when in College.

He did, on occasion, intervene in College affairs. In particular, when a change in Statutes was proposed (and eventually carried) which he thought ill-considered and ill-argued, he wrote a letter to the Fellows, which ended: 'Caius is a noble college, cared for by generations of noble men. Time, no doubt, brings all nobility to dust, but I do not think we are called upon to assist in the demolition of that which has no grounds of dissolution within itself.'

Oakeshott was remarkably handsome as a young man, and retained an astonishing distinction of appearance into extreme old age. As Aubrey said of Hobbes: 'He was no woman hater.' He married three times. He was once proposed for the Mastership. The Fellow who proposed him spoke eloquently, and alluded, with some delicacy, to the unspoken objection in the minds of some of the older Fellows: 'He is not, at present, married, but he is not unacquainted with the matrimonial condition.'

That he was, in life and by conviction, a Romantic is beyond dispute. His lifelong polemic against the Managerial State was also a positive sense of life's adventure. The highest virtue for him seems to have been an intelligent readiness to cope with the contingencies of life. Any political philosophy which aims to reduce the element of adventure – and hence the need for courage – from human life was to be deplored. He did, after all, celebrate 'younger sons making their way in a world that has little place for them, footloose adventurers who left the land to take to trade'. And his heroes included the intellectually audacious Abelard, Benvenuto Cellini, St John of the Cross, and, above all, Montaigne.

When someone would make a remark in conversation 'I think X' – 'X' being some doubtful or even crass proposition – Michael would reply, with exquisitely non-committal courtesy: 'Oh, *do* you, *do* you?' So habitual was this turn of phrase with him, that I have found myself fancying that had he been Moses, hearing the voice from the Burning Bush proclaim 'I am that I am', he would have replied – with real interest – 'Oh, *are* you, *are* you, *are* you?'

He was a living disproof of the idea that modern philosophy must inevitably become an arid, technical discipline. He did not strike his friends (as Wittgenstein certainly struck his friends) as a perturbed spirit – for he was fortunate in having a happy disposition. But, as with Wittgenstein, the philosophical spirit pervaded even his most ordinary talk. In his late eighties he used regularly to attend a College dining society, now named after him, where he would sit up into the small hours enchanting the undergraduates with his conversation. They were certainly not all intellectuals: but he was, in his unpompous way, initiating them into 'the conversation of mankind' – whether they realised it or not.

A young composer once asked him what was the most important thing in life, and he replied 'To live gaily!' He used the word in its old sense – of course. And he meant it.

5

The Poetics of the Civil Life

Timothy Fuller

Michael Oakeshott was born on December 11, 1901, in the county of Kent, and died on December 19, 1990, at his nineteenth-century quarryman's cottage, on the edge of the Purbeck marble quarries, in the tiny village of Acton on the Dorset coast. His academic career began at Cambridge in the early 1920s. He was a Life Fellow of Gonville & Caius College where his portrait now presides over the faculty dining room, and he remained a university lecturer in history until the end of the 1940s with an interlude of military service in the Second World War. Following a brief time at Oxford he took the Professorship of Political Science at the London School of Economics in 1951.

The latter appointment, at the time, was a matter of much political gossip. The Churchill government had been thrown out of office in 1945, but then the Tories and Churchill regained power just as the chair in political science, previously held by the very prominent and socialist Harold Laski, became vacant. The appointment of the conservative Oakeshott to a post at the heart of the university in Britain most famous for its association with Sidney and Beatrice Webb and the Fabian Socialists, was a scandal among the intelligentsia. For years, many British academics disdained Oakeshott as a political appointee. And they were not reassured by his inaugural lecture, 'Political Education', which has become a celebrated example of the sceptical attitude to politics reminiscent of the essays of David Hume or Michel de Montaigne. In that lecture, Oakeshott rejected the politics of infinite progress through the propagation of ideological programmes for the radical transformation of the human condition. In particular, he insisted it was not the vocation of the political philosopher to change the world but to understand it.

In saying this, Oakeshott was challenging Marx's dictum in the 'Theses on Feuerbach' that the purpose of modern thought was not to explain but to change the world. Marx had set himself up as a court of appeal, ruling on philosophic schools as to whether they were revolutionary or good as opposed to reactionary or bad. From the perspective of a Marx-influenced intellectual environment Oakeshott inevitably was seen as a reactionary.

What has become clear since then, however, particularly as the influence of Marxist categories has been increasingly challenged, is that Oakeshott was not at all interested in going back to an earlier state of affairs. His conservative disposition was quite far removed from any nostalgic reaction, or from any neo-conservative or neo-liberal counter-ideology. Thus he never really became the guru of Thatcherism as some who lack subtlety have alleged.

What he meant was that each generation must do the best it can with the resources it has in responding to circumstances it did not choose but cannot avoid. The idea that we are better than our forebears he thought pretentious and proved largely by self-affirmation. In his view of the human condition, the delights of life are seldom to be found by continually seeking to transpose everything into a goal-oriented project. Conservatism to him meant enjoying the possibilities of the present, the only time one has actually got to do something with. He deplored, for example, the politicisation of the universities because he saw that it would rob students of the one brief interval in life when they could explore the delights of learning for its own sake without the burdens of immediate practical responsibility.

He had little brief for the current preoccupation with 'leadership' and 'problem-solving', and little praise for the lingering influence of Benthamite calculation. The view

5. The Poetics of the Civil Life

that life's meaning is always to be found in the quest for some future condition, putatively superior to the present, he found a sad misunderstanding of what it means to be human.

For years after his inaugural, critics accused him of pessimism or even nihilism. This response signified to Oakeshott that we live in a peculiarly faithless age. He meant that the nihilism is actually lodged in those who cannot find value in the present life, or anywhere but in politics, but must always seek some other world. This represented to him a deep-seated denial of life's meaning expressed paradoxically as a quest for a meaning which is not yet. By contrast he lauded the poet for delighting in the beauty of images, the composer who thinks in melodic lines. I shall soon try to illustrate this idea of his a bit more.

Oakeshott was the most significant British political philosopher of our century and yet, like Montaigne, for whom he had the greatest admiration, a man of specific locality and an idiosyncratic turn of mind. Oakeshott was in the modern world, and one of its most profound analysts, but not of it. His cottage had no central heating or television and only recently a telephone. The advantages of these amenities he thought exaggerated, perhaps not altogether good for us. To the last, he corresponded in a tiny, rather elegant script, disdaining the typewriter, much less the word-processor.

Oakeshott surveyed the world without feeling compelled to roam it. He had a great attachment to certain places in the world – the France of Montaigne, Siena, the mountains of Colorado, Cambridge, or Winchester Cathedral which he sometimes stopped to visit when travelling between London and Dorset – but he felt no necessity to go to them. He had a clear vision of these places from afar, and that was sufficient. He had no interest in photographs, and to my knowledge never took a snapshot in his life.

Seeking to understand himself, he welcomed travellers to his cottage whose conversation would complement his own and check his observations. In writing, his genre was the essay which in his case, as Emerson said of Montaigne's essays, was the transfer of conversations to the written page. What he wrote he saw as invitations to his readers to respond conversationally, not as arguments seeking to end all argument. He thought his essays merely revealed the reasons he had come to accept for the views he took. He easily admitted that others might see things differently. Civility, the mark of humanity, was the acknowledgment of the uncertainty of all human knowing. His essays carry on a tradition in English letters we associate with the names of Bacon, Hume, Macaulay and John Stuart Mill.

He was a shrewd judge of character and yet he had a romantic streak. His judgments seldom turned judgmental, and he regularly preferred to serve those who might reasonably have been expected to serve him. He did not look for reasons to be negative.

Friendship and love were central to his life. The relationship of friends, he said, 'is dramatic, not utilitarian'. Loving is not doing good, nor is it a duty, but the communication of one unique self to another: 'Neither merit nor necessity has any part in the generation of love; its progenitors are chance and choice – chance because what cannot be identified in advance cannot be sought; and in choice the inescapable practical component of desire makes itself felt.'[1]

Encounters with him were dramatic but not melodramatic, memorable but not at the price of one's composure. He led his life as if he knew friendship and love were to be found, and yet he was always joyfully surprised when they came his way. It is hard to imagine that he ever appraised anyone in terms of their potential usefulness to himself.

The phrase 'chance and choice' occurs elsewhere in Oakeshott's writings only in relation to his definition of politics as attending to the arrangements of a set of people 'whom chance or choice have brought together'. The connotations of the phrase differ from love to politics, but what is implicit in both is his view of life as an adventure fraught with contingency and encompassed in mystery. He transposed the idea of pilgrimage in the religious and

---

[1] 'The Voice of Poetry in the Conversation of Mankind' (1959) in *Rationalism in Politics*, p. 244.

5. The Poetics of the Civil Life

chivalric senses into the drama of self-discovery. Biblical language was never far from his thought, particularly those myths which most vividly and imaginatively evoked the human condition.

Most powerful for him was that Genesis story on which, in fact, he published two different essays thirty-five years apart (1948 and 1983), calling both 'The Tower of Babel'. This was the biblical source of his scepticism. He found that story a most relevant comment on modern rationalism which he disdained not alone by comparison to Platonic and Scholastic rationalism, but especially by comparison to his view that life is a traveller's tale. There is a course to follow, but with no simple or certain destination. His models were as diverse as *Sir Gawain and the Green Knight, Amadis of Gaul, Don Quixote*, Montaigne's *Essays*, Shakespeare's romances, J.H. Shorthouse's *John Inglesant*, Walter Pater's *Gaston de la Tour*, Willa Cather's *My Antonia*, Joseph Conrad's sea stories, cowboy stories of the Old West and the tales of Isak Dinesen.

In a little-read essay, 'Leviathan: A Myth' (1947), Oakeshott revealed the tie of his lifelong interest in Hobbes – the one major thinker on whom he wrote extensively – to the religious imagination that was distinctively his:

> The myth of the Fall of Man, says Berdyaev, 'is at bottom a proud idea ... If man fell away from God, he must have been an exalted creature, endowed with great freedom and power'. But in the myth of our civilisation as it appears in *Leviathan* the emphasis is on the opposite pole; it recalls man to his littleness, his imperfection, his mortality ... what makes *Leviathan* a masterpiece of philosophical literature is the profound logic of Hobbes's imagination, his power as an artist. Hobbes recalls us to our mortality with a deliberate conviction, with a subtle and sustained argument. He, with a sure and steady irony, does what Swift could do with only an intermittent brilliance, and what the literature of Existentialism is doing today with an exaggerated display of emotion and a false suggestion of novelty.[2]

---

[2] 'Leviathan: A Myth' (1949) in *Hobbes on Civil Association*, p. 153ff.

It is a mark of Oakeshott's originality to have seen Hobbes as a brilliant contributor to the organising myths of our civilisation and not merely as the prototype of modern secularism and rational choice.

Oakeshott thought egalitarian politics fallacious, but he was a spiritual democrat: he did not think anyone could gain exemption from the limits of mortal human existence; he was Augustinian, not Pelagian. He thought Hobbes a touchstone for our era which needed to be recalled both to the contingent character of its knowledge and to an admission of its mortality:

> The pursuit of perfection as the crow flies is an activity both impious and unavoidable in human life. It involves the penalties of impiety (the anger of the gods and social isolation), and its reward is not that of achievement but that of having made the attempt. It is an activity, therefore, suitable for individuals, but not for societies. For an individual who is impelled to engage in it, the reward may exceed both the penalty and the inevitable defeat. The penitent may hope, or even expect, to fall back a wounded hero, into the arms of an understanding and forgiving society. And even the impenitent can be reconciled with himself in the powerful necessity of his impulse, though, like Prometheus, he must suffer for it. For a society, on the other hand, the penalty is a chaos of conflicting ideals, the disruption of a common life, and the reward is the renown which attaches to monumental folly.[3]

While rejecting talk of a 'human nature', Oakeshott none the less affirmed the abiding presence of something categorically human that does not differ now from what it was in the past. Like Aristotle, Oakeshott insisted the distinctiveness of being human manifests itself in the faculty of conversation:

> As civilised human beings, we are the inheritors, neither of an inquiry about ourselves and the world, nor of an accumulating body of information, but of a conversation, begun in the primeval forests and extended and made more

[3] 'The Tower of Babel' (1948) in *Rationalism in Politics*, p. 59ff.

5. The Poetics of the Civil Life

articulate in the course of centuries ... It is the ability to participate in this conversation, and not the ability to reason cogently, to make discoveries about the world, or to contrive a better world, which distinguishes the human being from the animal and the civilised man from the barbarian.[4]

In short, we have been fully human from that primeval moment when human beings discovered their humanity by sitting down to talk. The civilised are those anywhere who know this; the barbarians are those anywhere who resist knowing it. Yet, as conversational beings, we are endlessly implicated in an engagement of self-discovery and association; we have a history, he thought, not a nature. Doctrines and orthodoxies are always to be adjusted to new conditions; ideologies come and go, for they are momentary coagulations in the fluid sea of human utterance, caricatures of a complex reality. They crystallise only to dissolve, and they will never satisfactorily substitute for, nor exhaust the revelations of, the masterpieces of religious, political, poetic and scientific thinking. The latter, in their probing revelations of the human predicament, resist all efforts to be reduced to textbooks or 'solutions' to 'problems'.

Similarly, human beings are in principle free: to be human, Oakeshott thought, is to be a reflective intelligence interpreting the surrounding circumstances and responding in accordance with what one understands or misunderstands the character – the possibilities and the limitations – of those circumstances to be. Human beings must learn everything. We are what we learn to become. We find ourself born into a world already shaped by those who came before us and who seem to understand what we have yet to understand. We must appropriate that world to ourselves as best we can, and no one can do it for us.[5]

In elaborating Oakeshott's political outlook, it is necessary to see what is often missed by commentators: his outlook is suffused with a religious character that yields no easy doctrinal formulations because its motive is not to

---

[4] 'The Voice of Poetry in the Conversation of Mankind' (1959) in *Rationalism in Politics*, p. 199.
[5] *On Human Conduct* (first essay) (1975); 'A Place of Learning' (1974).

construct propositions. His inspiration is the pre-Reformation religious imagination of popular Christianity filtered through the romantic expression of nineteenth-century poetics:

> Religious faith is the evocation of a sentiment (the love, the glory, or the honour of God, for example, or even a humble *caritas*), to be added to all others as the motive of all motives in terms of which the fugitive adventures of human conduct, without being released from their mortal and their moral conditions, are graced with an intimation of immortality: the sharpness of death and the deadliness of doing overcome, and the transitory sweetness of a mortal affection, the tumult of a grief and the passing beauty of a May morning recognised neither as merely evanescent adventures nor as emblems of better things to come, but as *aventures*, themselves encounters with eternity.[6]

In passages such as these, Oakeshott's distinctive appreciation, and affirmation, of the human shines through. His view of politics, numerous critics of a certain kind notwithstanding, bespoke neither pessimism nor nihilism. The most often quoted passage on this point is this:

> In political activity, then, men sail a boundless and bottomless sea; there is neither harbour for shelter nor floor for anchorage, neither starting-place nor appointed destination. The enterprise is to keep afloat on an even keel; the sea is both friend and enemy; and the seamanship consists in using the resources of a traditional manner of behaviour in order to make a friend of every hostile occasion.[7]

Juxtaposing the latter with his evocation of the encounter with eternity, one sees that, fascinated though he was by the study of politics, Oakeshott found the heart of life elsewhere. Oakeshott is the pre-eminent antagonist of all those today who wish to reduce the meaning of life to political action. The fatality of the political life, he thought, is that it is always tempted to think of acting once and for

---

[6] *On Human Conduct*, p. 85.
[7] 'Political Education' (1951) in *Rationalism in Politics*, p. 127.

5. The Poetics of the Civil Life

all, perhaps for the last time. In the nature of things, however, this is what politics can never do, and what it would hate if it ever actually verged on doing it. Politics must thrive on its own dissatisfaction, seeking that completion which would be the final contradiction of what makes the activity attract to begin with.

If this is not precisely the Augustinian doctrine of the two cities, it is nevertheless a comparable imagining of the faultlines of our existence: we are caught between contemplation and delight on the one hand and the 'deadliness of doing', 'the *danse macabre* of wants and satisfactions', on the other. Insofar as this differs from Augustine's formulation, it is because Oakeshott derived from Hegel the engagement to avoid the appearance of dualism in characterising human experience, believing, as did Hegel, that the modern world was distinguished by the task to refuse the estrangement of the spiritual and the material. For Oakeshott, this meant that the modalities of experience were encompassed in the unity of experience as a whole; every way of knowing is a way of being in the world – we are in ourselves what we are for ourselves. To grasp historical existence – the meeting of time and eternity – would involve comprehending Hegel chastened by Augustine. This is a project, ultimately theological in nature, which Oakeshott long thought of pursuing but never undertook.

Politics is a necessary evil, neither to be despised nor overrated. That Oakeshott did not take his bearings there is a deficiency only for those who do not share his quest for the poetic intimations of life amidst an otherwise drab activism.

It is in this sense that Oakeshott was willing to call himself a 'conservative'. All the important activities, he argued, are inherently conservative because they depend not only on acquiring an abstract technique but also on apprenticeship to practitioners who exhibit in their work the background lore or art of the activity which cannot be written down in books or summarised in manuals. The mistake of modern rationalists was to think that the technical part of knowledge could stand by itself, and here he took a view reminiscent of Michael Polanyi's explorations of tacit and personal knowledge.

He was often criticised for insisting on the importance of tradition, and criticised in some quarters as an historicist. Others have asserted that he could not distinguish between the mere givenness of a background and the affirmation of it as good, that he drifted off into some sort of traditionalist mysticism. Oakeshott was seldom given to responding to these criticisms. He might have said that the issue of what is virtuous in our heritage arises out of a discussion conducted in terms of that heritage and by appeal to it. How else is this to take place? He did not see this as a 'problem' to which there may be a 'solution', or no solution. It is a description of being human that our resources are both inspiring and limiting at the same time.

Thus a conservative disposition followed from recognising what the human situation is. Oakeshott was not urging us to be conservative – he was arguing that we could not help but be so. To deny this is not only to disguise the truth about ourselves, but also to lead us into ill-considered projects for transforming the human race. He sought to derive no specific political programme from this disposition, and he was often sceptical of those programmatic conservatives and neo-conservatives whom he characterised as devising 'plans to end all planning'. Here he remained consistent with what he understood to be the philosopher's vocation to speak in the indicative, not the hortatory, mood: 'Thinking is at first associated with an extraneous desire for action. And it is some time, perhaps, before we discern that philosophy is without any direct bearing upon the practical conduct of life, and that it has certainly never offered its true followers anything which could be mistaken for a gospel.'[8] 'A philosophical essay', he said, 'does not dissemble the conditionality of the conclusions it throws up and although it may enlighten it does not instruct. It is, in short, a well-considered intellectual adventure recollected in tranquillity.'[9]

As a political sceptic he could accept the principle that that government is best which governs least. His best

---

[8] *Experience and its Modes*, p. 1.
[9] *On Human Conduct*, p. vii.

5. The Poetics of the Civil Life

government would be one which devised procedural rules, adjudicated disputes when necessary, and had few or no economic resources to distribute, thus leaving it with little power to preach instead of govern.

He thought that the main obstacle to enjoying such a government was the unavoidable and continuous preparation for war that imposed upon all modern governments the undertaking to organise society in terms of uniformity of goals, reinforced by infatuation with technology, and the belief that human beings could not be entrusted to take care of themselves unless directed by an extrinsic goal or purpose, an ideology.

Yet he has also been called a classic 'liberal'.[10] There is much warrant for this view in that it points to his belief in the importance of the individual, of self-reliance, of property rights, of dispersal of governmental power and of the rule of law.[11]

In fact, Oakeshott combined elements of both conservatism and liberalism in his thought. He was not a doctrinaire thinker. He thought he dwelled in a tradition of thinking comprising many nuances. It did not occur to him that one should choose among abstract positions. He was both an individualist and a traditionalist, finding them essential complements. The most careful working out of this is the Second Essay of *On Human Conduct* wherein he explicates how individuals, by subscribing to 'practices', associate themselves with others in terms of a manner of thinking and doing – a language – which gives them an idiom in which to express their talents, but not a command as to what they are to do or to say.

The most famous distinction to emerge from Oakeshott's culminating work, *On Human Conduct* (1975), is that between 'enterprise association' and 'civil association'. Briefly, the former is a voluntary agreement among individuals to associate in the pursuit of a common purpose or purposes. In this sort of association, the individuals

---

[10] Most recently by Paul Franco in *The Political Philosophy of Michael Oakeshott* (1990).
[11] 'The Political Economy of Freedom' (1949) in *Rationalism in Politics* and 'The Rule of Law' in *On History and Other Essays* (1983).

become role-players, subordinating themselves to the requirements of succeeding in the chosen pursuit, usually under a manager whose function is to coordinate a division of labour effectively. For Oakeshott, enterprises are intrinsically private activities – even if they involve many or all of the people in a society – because they are associations organised in terms of someone's chosen goal or purpose which is not what others might choose. In principle, then, it should be voluntary precisely because what it chooses as its organising principle cannot be what everyone would choose, and it must exclude other possible pursuits that do not fit its ambitions.

Civil association, by contrast, is 'an intelligent relationship enjoyed only in being learned and understood, distinguished (for example) from relationship in terms of propinquity, kinship, genes ...' and in which citizens would be associated 'neither in respect of a common enterprise nor in procuring the responses of others in seeking the satisfaction of their individual wants, but in terms of a practice or language of civil intercourse which they have not designed or chosen but within the jurisdiction of which they recognise themselves to fall and which, in subscribing to it, they continuously explore and reconstitute'.[12]

Oakeshott's ideal commonwealth is 'not itself an enterprise, an undertaking, an "economy", or an educational or therapeutic organisation, and not enterprisers or groups of enterprisers associated in seeking recognition or advantage for themselves in their undertakings, but an association of *cives*; a relationship of equals, and a self-sufficient condition in being relationship in terms of the conditions of a practice which are not used up in being used and not in terms of a substantive purpose or purposes to be pursued.'

In developing these ideas, Oakeshott had also to turn his attention to the nature of authority, of law, and of civil obligation as they would appear in such an ideal civil association. The civil association requires someone to occupy an office of authority that is acknowledged as the source of authoritative pronouncements by those who have

---

[12] *On Human Conduct*, pp. 182-3.

5. The Poetics of the Civil Life

subscribed to it. The occupant of an office like this is not privileged with special insight or knowledge, and is certainly not warranted in defining the *summum bonum*. The one who exercises authority is to establish and clarify rules or laws in what Oakeshott called the adverbial form: they are considerations to be taken into account in choosing how to conduct ourselves with each other. 'They are not the rules of a game' for that would imply we are already engaged in a common pursuit and more or less repetitive performance. They are not the rules of an enterprise because the rules of an enterprise 'specify conditions alleged to be instrumental to the pursuit of what is already recognised as a common purpose'.[13] They are rules which 'prescribe the common responsibilities (and the counterpart "rights" to have these responsibilities fulfilled) of agents and in terms of which they put by their characters as enterprisers and put by all that differentiates them from one another and recognise themselves as formal equals – *cives*'.[14]

Thus there will always be disputes as to how to subscribe to the rules in the specific actions we choose in our particular circumstances. There must be authority to make rules and to adjudicate disputes over the rules. But none of this implies for Oakeshott development towards common purposes or the elaboration of a managerial policy for relating people to each other efficiently. Adjudication presupposes adherence to the rule of law in the sense defined and is to amplify our understanding of what the law says. This must be done significantly in that it furthers our understanding; justifiably in that a decision must be connected to the law which the adjudication presupposes; appropriately in being the resolution of a specific contingent uncertainty as to what adequate subscription to the law means in a specific case; and durably because it enters into the system of law intelligibly for citizens in deciding their future conduct.[15] Obligations, as opposed to actions taken out of a sense of moral duty, derive from the recognition of the law as authentic, and the law's validity 'is

[13] Ibid., p. 128.
[14] Ibid.
[15] Ibid., p. 133.

a matter to be decided in terms of the resources for decision' provided by the law,[16] and by the continuous reaffirmation of its validity over time on the part of citizens who can distinguish between calculations of personal advantage or disadvantage and relating to each other in a strictly moral or civil relationship: as mutual subscribers to a system of rules that qualify their conduct without imposing specific actions. This is the public realm strictly speaking, detached from distraction by the numerous private pursuits of enterprise relationships.

But all of this does not fully reveal his commitment to and felicity in teaching. The original impetus to his academic career was his admiration for his teachers at St George's School in Hertfordshire. He always thought of himself, first, as a learner, but those of us who saw him at work lecturing or in seminars knew that here was an extraordinary teacher. Even in his seventies, when he limited himself to attending the general seminar in the History of Political Thought at the London School of Economics, and occasionally reading papers on the idea of history, he could identify with students in a special way. He was less put off by the machinations of student politics than many an academic who would be thought to be more 'liberal'. In a way, he operated as if the university were the civil association the modern state has never quite become.

He had an enormous appreciation of the young and never forgot what it was to be young: 'Everybody's young days are a dream, a delightful insanity, a sweet solipsism. Nothing in them has a fixed shape, nothing a fixed price; everything is a possibility, and we live happily on credit. There are no obligations to be observed; there are no accounts to be kept. Nothing is specified in advance; everything is what can be made of it. The world is a mirror in which we seek the reflection of our own desires ... urgency is our criterion of importance; and we do not easily understand that what is humdrum need not be despicable. We are impatient of

---

[16] Ibid., p. 151.

5. The Poetics of the Civil Life

restraint; and we readily believe, like Shelley, that to have contracted a habit is to have failed ...'[17]

I have not personally known anyone who could feel the beauty of youth more intensely even at the end of his days than Oakeshott. The sense of being alive to the possibilities of existence was with him to the end, and it was the secret of his effect on students. He never forgot what it was like for them even though he knew, what too many teachers recently have avoided knowing, that one cannot remain in the youthful dream: 'For most there is what Conrad called the "shadow line" which, when we pass it, discloses a solid world of things, each with its fixed shape, each with its own point of balance, each with its price; a world of fact, not poetic image, in which what we have spent on one thing we cannot spend on another; a world inhabited by others besides ourselves who cannot be reduced to mere reflections of our own emotions'.[18]

The essential works to read are *Experience and its Modes* (1933), *Rationalism in Politics* (1962; new and expanded edition 1991), *On Human Conduct* (1975), *Hobbes on Civil Association* (1975), *On History and Other Essays* (1983), *The Voice of Liberal Learning* (1989).

As I list these, I remember that one of Oakeshott's favourite stories was of the Chinese wheelwright who could not, at seventy, turn over his craft to his son because his son could not get the hang of it. The wheelwright generalised from his failure to inculcate into his son more than the abstract rules of his craft when he remarked to his Duke, who was reading the words of the sages, that books are 'the lees and scum of bygone men'. 'All that was worth handing on,' the wheelwright said, 'died with them; the rest, they put in their books.' One thinks too of Socrates who refused to write philosophy down. But then one remembers also Plato who devised a method for writing it down without writing it down. The intent of Oakeshott's writing was like that. In the lees and scum there is, after all, perhaps a lingering presence which is a blessing in disguise.

---

[17] 'On Being Conservative' (1956) in *Rationalism in Politics*, p. 195.
[18] Ibid., p. 196.

6

The Civilised Imperative

Jeffrey Hart

Michael Oakeshott established modesty as a philosophical principle, and extended it to many other modes of discourse. In his work, indeed, modesty is a category of being. At the same time, and not at all paradoxically, he was a towering figure. It is notable that Noel Annan in his memoir *Our Age* portrays Oakeshott as a 'deviant' from the conventional wisdom of the 1920-1950 'age'. In so deviating, he was the most important political thinker in the Anglo-Saxon tradition since Burke, and I have not overlooked J.S. Mill.

Michael Oakeshott was the guest of honour at *National Review's* twentieth-anniversary celebration, the proceedings that year taking place in two parts. First was an address by Oakeshott at Hunter College, and later a banquet, with speeches, at the Plaza Hotel.

When we received at *National Review* the paper Oakeshott was to deliver at Hunter College, it proved to be unexpectedly abstruse and abstract. All previous Oakeshott had not only been splendidly lucid and concrete in its terms but stylistically potent. In philosophy, Oakeshott was the finest stylist since William James. I have mentioned Burke earlier, and it is important that Burke's first major work was a treatise on aesthetics. Oakeshott wrote memorably on poetry – meaning 'literature' or 'rhetoric' – as one of the voices or modes of experience. It was a non-abstracting mode, in contrast to the voice of science. Style, thus, was an embodiment of Oakeshott's idea of voices and modes. One

6. The Civilised Imperative

recalls that he was an early contributor to F.R. Leavis' *Scrutiny*.

But what were we to make at *National Review* of the paper he had sent us? With almost a straight face, and in tones of comprehensive kindness, the late James Burnham turned the problem over to me. 'In the journals of philosophy,' he said, 'it is customary in the case of difficult papers for the editor to provide a brief summary from time to time of what has just been said. I wonder if you will do this for our publication of this paper in *National Review*.'

Well, yes, I would; and I was even assigned to ask the first question of Oakeshott in a panel discussion following his address at Hunter.

Leaving the auditorium at Hunter College, and on the way to the Plaza, I heard a woman say, 'That was Buckley's greatest hoax. That wasn't Michael Oakeshott. That was an actor playing a philosopher.'

And yet difficult and abstract as that paper was, it adumbrated one of Oakeshott's major contributions to political clarification. His shift toward abstract generalisation moved what had previously been implicit, as in *Rationalism in Politics* (1962), to the level of general theory. This became crystallised in *On Human Conduct* (1975), which proposed a theory of the state which came down to earth in the practice of Margaret Thatcher; and which is enshrined in the much neglected 'limited government' Tenth Amendment to the US Constitution.

Oakeshott rejected managerial government in favour of civil association. It was Kenneth Minogue, I think, who coined the term 'teleocracy' or government-with-a-mission. Such a government has goals and seeks the power to impose them. Such goals are usually derived from theories or ideals. Oakeshott thought that a civil association was far preferable. In it government would be a neutral umpire, administering neutral rules of behaviour, within which the citizens pursued their own goals. The social order would amount to an unending series of adjustments and exchanges, with no overall plan or goal or system, except the fostering by individuals of existence at the highest civilised level.

Oakeshott's political theory, or, more correctly, teaching, was thus anti-perfectionist. Goals and programmes were an effort by government to move human nature up a notch, or several notches. Oakeshott saw politics as a mode of protecting and adjusting customary forms of behaviour, which rested upon experience. As editor of the *Cambridge Journal*, he rejected not only the Labour Party socialist teleocracy but also the Tory paternalism of R.A. Butler and Harold Macmillan, the 'wets' of their day. Such Tories were saying, considered Oakeshott, that they could run the teleocracy more efficiently than Clement Attlee. Oakeshott loathed a politics that would impose from above new and unexperienced forms of behaviour.

Hovering in the background of Oakeshott's writing are the great sceptics – sceptics, that is, about the possibility of certain knowledge: Hume, Montaigne, Pascal, Cervantes. And, of course, Burke; though the final adjudication of Burke's scepticism, perhaps deep, remains a matter open to serious investigation. Oakeshott's scepticism, in practice, was not an enervating but an animating force. It was first outlined in his *Experience and its Modes* (1933), a brilliant philosophical work and also a curiosity which fused scepticism with the idealist tradition which comes down ultimately from Plato.

In *Rationalism in Politics*, Oakeshott's scepticism pointed towards Burke. What is 'knowledge'?

> Technical knowledge can be learned from a book; it can be learned in a correspondence course. Moreover, much of it can be learned by heart, repeated by rote and applied mechanically ... On the other hand, practical knowledge can neither be taught nor learned, but only imparted and acquired. It exists only in practice, and the only way to acquire it is by apprenticeship to a master, not because the master can teach it (he cannot) but because it can be acquired only by continuous contact with one who is perpetually practising it.[1]

I must say that though I agree with this theory of knowledge, Oakeshott's language here suggests too much

---

[1] *Rationalism in Politics* (1962), pp. 10–11.

6. The Civilised Imperative

an *atelier* or iron-forge. Surely T.S. Eliot was 'in continuous contact' with 'master(s)' when he absorbed himself in Dante and the other great practitioners of his craft. Oakeshott would surely concede the point. But his own point is sound. Practical knowledge is an activity. In his *Reflections*, discussing the reasons for removing King James II in 1688, Burke takes as his hero Lord Somers, the 'statesman', who through long practical experience of statecraft 'knew' that King James had to be removed – but preserved as much of political tradition as he could in so doing.

One might well say that Burke, with Oakeshott following, discovered the 'unconscious' in society, what the Romans called a *habitus*. The virtuous life of the citizen is not a matter of rules printed in a book, but a matter of absorbing a whole way of life. (It would be a valuable endeavour to read the so-called great books, the books that continue to matter as reflections of the accumulated experience of ways of life.)

When Michael Oakeshott replaced Harold Laski in 1951 as Professor of Political Science at the London School of Economics, his accession was felt to be a momentous event. Laski had been a foremost spokesman for the old socialism, a pamphleteering teleocrat *par excellence*. At his inaugural address, as Annan records, Oakeshott's LSE students were appalled. Oakeshott told them that their hopes for a better world were an illusion and that their guides had been charlatans.

The term 'post-modern' today means many things, but it has a particular application to Oakeshott. His scepticism, his sense of natural limits and of the human scale, freed him from the modern experience of *Angst* and alienation, which are in fact the obverse of a hunger for utopian perfection. Like his hero Montaigne, he had emotions that were overwhelmingly positive. Late at night, as the *National Review* anniversary proceedings were winding down at the Plaza Hotel, I heard Michael Oakeshott whisper to a pretty young woman, 'Just call me Mickey.'

I am unable to establish at the moment when Oakeshott began regularly to attend Church of England services, appreciating the liturgy to the degree that he turned towards Jerusalem at the proper moment. I doubt that he 'believed' in God, but I judge, provisionally, that he believed in a *habitus*, the accumulated wisdom of one of the voices or modes of experience – in this case, the Church of England.

In his late eighties Oakeshott became the centre of a dining, drinking and discussion society in Caius College, Cambridge, sitting into the small hours with the young men. His conversation had a curiously innocent, even child-like quality, often very humorous. He taught his friends that every question was open in the great conversation of mind. His theory of knowledge was 'practical' in practice. He embodied the practical knowledge of civilisation, was a 'verray parfit gentil knicht'. He died at his home in Acton, Dorset on December 19, 1990, aged 89.

7

The History of Political Thought Seminar

Kenneth Minogue

The Master's degree seminar in the History of Political Thought, starring Michael Oakeshott, has become widely recognised as a notable academic institution. It had distinguished visitors, and many of its students went on to academic success, but above all perhaps it was the workshop in which Oakeshott developed many of the formulations which later appeared in *On History and Other Essays* (1983). Yet the seminar was not Michael Oakeshott's natural habitat, and students in the 1950s at the London School of Economics had sometimes grumbled that he did not hold a regular graduate seminar. He always preferred the informality of conversation to the self-consciousness of academic discussion. His main teaching activity at the School in the decade after his appointment in 1951 (apart from supervising graduates and undergraduates) was lecturing on the history of political thought. Then fate took a hand. In about 1960 the University of London set up a scheme of one-year Master's degrees. Convenient for economists and practitioners of other technical subjects, who could always put an extra year to good use, this innovation was virtually an embarrassment in more discursive subjects. One year threatened, in practice, to reduce to the nine months between October and June, a threat to which historians and others responded by scheduling the examinations in September. Their students were thus doomed to spending the summer in the libraries, and failing to get their results before the autumn in which they were launched upon the next stage of their careers. Still, overseas students, especially American, found the one-year MSc a useful diversion on their way to graduate research.

Oakeshott characteristically responded to this administrative *dictat* by making the best of things. In devising a course his principle was to find a point of entry quite different from anything students would have met in their undergraduate study, and he found it in focusing on the assumptions of intellectual history. Academic imitation and problem convergence is such that innovations of this kind rapidly lose their novelty; method in intellectual history now enjoys a vogue it did not have then. In the seminar, each of the basic terms – history, thought, and politics, in that order – was subjected to sustained discussion at weekly meetings throughout the year. A slowly changing set of books was steadily digested. In addition students were required to study a text in depth, and to write an essay on some general topic under exam conditions. Elie Kedourie rabbinically trawling his way through the *Philosophy of Right* was one of the great theatrical experiences of those days. Kedourie was a regular presence at the seminar, as were Robert Orr and I. Ernest Thorp, John Charvet, Maurice Cranston, William and Shirley Letwin sometimes attended and gave papers. A changing cast of available luminaries in London at the time also alternated with student presentations, ranging from Robert Lane and Brough Macpherson to Quentin Skinner and John Pocock.

The central preoccupation of the seminar was entirely coloured by Oakeshott's own philosophy, for in it he returned to think and constantly rethink what history was. Until the later seventies he always gave a number of papers himself, and the end process of this developing thought finally appeared in 1983. *On History and Other Essays* is typical late-Oakeshott in that his earlier simplicity and wit is qualified by a determined attempt to block all possible misunderstanding, however densely qualified his style

7. The History of Political Thought Seminar

might have to become in order to do so. The actual seminar papers he gave were a good deal more conversable. The talk was inevitably dominated (in spite of frequent good intentions to the contrary) by the older members, and also by many graduate students who, being for one reason or another able to attend for several years running, had acquired confidence, and also some feel for the rules of this particular game.

Oakeshott was very good with students, always treating their comments and questions with the utmost courtesy. Absorbing a question, he would often take a puff on his cigarette and gaze into the far distance for a minute, and then say: 'You mean ...' The reformulation that followed was, inevitably, a good deal more profound than the original question, and sometimes bore little relation to it, but the flattered student would usually accept the switch, and what would emerge would be an interesting development of the topic in question. One of the most striking virtues of these responses was their exhibition of Oakeshott's fertility in finding exemplifications interesting in their own terms. Whether it was Zachary Brooke's brilliant reinterpretation of Canossa, or the barrister who had recently attempted to derive from Magna Carta the implication that a Black defendant could only be judged by a Black jury of his peers, Oakeshott was a dab hand at the pedagogic marriage of universal and particular.

His papers, on the other hand, presented a smooth surface which students often found difficult to fight their way into. Oakeshott characteristically began on the heights of the universal and slowly descended towards his central subject. He seldom made explicit reference to the existing literature on the subject, though he was usually familiar with it. Every paper was a wholly new attempt at a coherent and rounded account of the subject, the criticism of other positions usually emerging implicitly or in discussion. Nothing dangled for instant criticism to grasp. The only real way in was to ask: 'What exactly is it that we mean by ... the past (etc.) here?' Along these lines we would often succeed in getting down to the area where the postulates of history, practice or politics were to be found.

It was both problem and opportunity that Oakeshott was swimming not only against the current of social science, but of common sense itself. The past 'as it actually was' in the imagination of Ranke, the average man, and the average philosopher such as A.J. Ayer, was dissolved, as a result of Oakeshott's relentlessly epistemological attentions, into a set of inferences drawn from present artifacts, themselves recognised as performances within a certain language or idiom, but capable of yielding historical interpretation in almost any sphere on which the historian might concentrate: a love letter, for example, might reveal something about the history of philosophical argument, a piece of sculpture about politics, and so on. What was generally revealed was far from anything the performer had intended to reveal. The last thing a historian was looking for was a direct narrative voice telling him what had actually happened; in these sophisticated terms the fashionable concern with bias is simpleminded.

Common sense is often parsimonious with categories and generous with values; Oakeshott went in the reverse direction. Faced with *The Revolution Betrayed* or *Our Island Story* he would refuse to regard them as bad or 'biased' history. They were simply not history at all. They were political utterances cast in the form of a description of notionally past events, and ought to be judged as such. Those who had read *Experience and its Modes* knew well that judging something in irrelevant terms was the very model for him of intellectual error. None the less whole generations of students passed through the seminar without ever quite understanding that 'it isn't history at all' is in no way a condemnatory judgment. It is in this way that sceptics can sometimes be reported as dogmatists.

The basic distinction on which this argument rested was that between a historical and a practical past. When Hollywood made a film about the French revolution, or a lawyer delved into some long-established property rights, or a politician referred to Canute and the waves, or to Nelson putting the telescope to his blind eye, the past was being used merely as decor; it served present purposes and in no way represented an attempt to understand some passage of past life. The expression 'Canute' might refer either to an uplifting fable, or to an eleventh-century Anglo-Norwegian king, and context determined its significance. To treat the expression as referring to one single object about which true and false statements are made was for Oakeshott the very model of a narrowing practical attitude. History is a complex practice arising from asking, and persisting in asking, certain types of questions about present objects, and is in no way licensed, as one might say, to correct other uses that might be made by people not engaged in historical investigation of these expressions.

Oakeshott never doubted that actual historical writing is somewhat miscellaneous, and that it often contains political argument and other modes of looking at the world. What he sought was to isolate the specifically historical and to exhibit it as a certain type of enquiry. Typically, he could only do this by thinking about types of understanding in general, and his eventual solution to this problem is to be found in the first essay of *On Human Conduct*. It is a matter of taking off from present experience and rising to what he called a 'conditional platform of understanding'.

In the early years of the seminar, this concern emerged in a phenomenology of understanding. In an era when the philosophy of science, bestriding the entire field of social science, focused attention on a single logic of explanation, Oakeshott was concerned with the different questions that might be asked about the world. What distinguished expounding from construing, diagnosing, the Democritean project of resolving complex wholes into their constituent parts, translating, classifying, etc.? Oakeshott always insisted that explanation ends in the unexplained or (more likely) the inexplicable. By continuing to ask the same type of question, a point would sooner or later be reached when the enquirer would run into final causes, or God. History in these terms began with a mystery rather than a problem, and the aim of the historian was to make it more intelligible by an assemblage of circumstances constituting an event. Each of these basic terms was closely examined.

A little later Oakeshott took to exploring this theme on the basis of German work on the character of theory. The

Greek metaphor from which the idea of theory emerged was visual. The *theôros* was a spectator sent to observe the religious festivals of other cities. *Thea* was an experience to be contemplated, *theôria* the enterprise of contemplating or inquiring, and *theôrêma* the theorem or product of this activity. Such an etymological taxonomy from a language better equipped for this investigation than English allowed Oakeshott to recast his distinctive view of what it is to understand something. A *thea* is already something identified, and is distinguished by its relative isolation. It cannot be absolutely distinguished from the *theôrêma* into which it might grow. Nevertheless, the movement towards a more theoretical understanding involves passing through a barrier in which the object of understanding changes its character. A theory of laughter, he observed, is no joke. It cannot be verified by trying it on someone and seeing if he laughs.

Understanding is thus a development of intelligibility, and it has no terminal point. In all thinking, except perhaps in mathematics, we simply exchange one puzzle for another. A favourite example was the development of Christian doctrine. An initial experience focused on Jesus had soon turned into a praxis: a notion that Christians ought to live in a certain manner. But in the next generation, this practice of faith, hope and charity had to be developed, partly for those who had never had the initial experiences, and partly because of the frustration of the hope of an imminent Second Coming. The exigencies of Roman citizenship also had to be accommodated. Before long, certainly with Augustine, the *parousia* (presence) had turned into a theorem about salvation and grace – a manner of thought quite unknown to the first generation. 'The odd thing about thinking,' Oakeshott once remarked, 'is its tremendous conatus to an inconvenient level of thought.' What it tends to generate is orthodoxy, a dogma: perhaps that is all that clarification means.

One of Oakeshott's basic concerns was to protect the valuable but limited insight of history (which he thought the key to understanding human affairs) from being destroyed by the blinding light of scientific laws, which

7. The History of Political Thought Seminar 93

could only distort our understanding of the human world. The dominant view of history in those days was the covering law theory of Carl Hempel and the Popperian view that history was just science with the laws left out. Hempel thought that the historian, in order to get from the fact that Louis XIV bankrupted his subjects by war to the fact that he died unpopular, must implicitly ride some such universal law as that kings who bankrupt their subjects die unpopular. A lot of time at the seminar was spent hammering this nonsense into the ground. But what was dissolved with it was the idea of a cause in history. Oakeshott agreed that historians used this term all the time, but he insisted that they could not possibly be talking about causes in any scientific sense, because such causes referred to necessary relations between abstract objects, and no such relations could rest on historical evidence. Gallie became a hero for making clear the fact that it is only when historians lack any real historical evidence for a connection that they have recourse to bits of theory from anthropology, psychoanalysis, sociology etc. Oakeshott sometimes compared the place of social science in history to the use of captions in silent movies: only invoked when the sequence of images could not tell its own story.

How then were historical events connected? The answer to this question can be found in the essays on historical events and historical change in *On History*. The basic answer, we have seen, is that the historian dissolves the mystery of his material by assembling circumstantial detail which fits together in such a way as to make an intelligible event. The prevailing metaphor in the later days of the seminar was that the historian was like the builder of a dry stone wall, adept at seeing how the materials lying to hand can be fitted together into a coherent shape. This metaphor should not be confused with that of a jigsaw puzzle, in which all the pieces must fit together in the one right combination. The doctrine explicitly takes off from Aristotle's treatment of contiguity in the *Physics* as an account of how things may be connected together merely by touching each other. Oakeshott was particularly keen to dissociate history from any of the accounts of change which assume an underlying structure of organic development, even though terms like 'evolution' and 'development' are commonly used to emphasise some element of pattern in the writings of actual historians. But the last thing 'the development of modern France' is, is a *development*: Oakeshott, like H.A.L. Fisher, belonged to the one damn thing after another school of historical understanding.

The same, almost deconstructionist, tendency to pluralise hard fixed identities led him to reject Lovejoy's idea of unit ideas. These powerful entities seemed to lead a life of their own and, originating perhaps in philosophy (as with the great chain of being) advance through the history of Western civilisation, hopping into poetry here or politics there, transforming theology in one place and throwing off little shoots, like science fiction, in another. Lovejoy's work supplied the seminar with all the joy of a luminous and unmistakable error, and he was accorded an appropriate status in its discussions. A certain amount of attention was accorded to the tendency of historians of political ideas to arraign earlier philosophers such as Plato, Rousseau and Hegel before the bar of morality. Here too was a practice of intellectual history which invoked hard nuggety ideas surviving intact the passage of time and context, and exerting a malign grip on human conduct. Real intellectual history, by contrast, was the history of men thinking, responding to their circumstances in terms of ideas which did indeed have an abstract and universal aspect, but which were never without a determining local colour. Levinson's account of *Confucian China and its Modern Fate* was a model of such work quite self-consciously undertaken, as was the work of Eric Stokes on the utilitarians in India.

The character of politics must necessarily be central to such an inquiry, and Oakeshott was always aware of 'that glassy film which tends to form when we have gazed too long at the world "politics" and wondered what it meant'. He regarded the term as a kind of albatross round the neck of clear thinking. Nobody ever had politics except polis-people, he once remarked, and added that the expression 'political thought' is an unfortunate nineteenth-century invention. But in any case, the historian is concerned not with a

7. The History of Political Thought Seminar

definition of politics which, being the abstract product of theory, would lose all connection with the contingencies which concern him. He is concerned simply with marks of recognition appropriate to the business he has in hand. That politics is a human activity, for example, is no very big jump of understanding. Bees and ants have no politics, and Caligula's horse is relevant because of Caligula's proposed nomination of it as a Senator and not because of its equinity. Politics must be recognised not only as a human activity, but also as a contingent one. Attempts to show that man is not properly human unless he engages in politics are philosophical rather than historical understandings. That politics is a realm in which a public sphere may be distinguished from a private was sometimes useful, but the word obviously has a multitude of uses, and Oakeshott sometimes quoted from the memoirs of a nineteenth-century British ambassador in Athens who had been robbed by the son of the Embassy's porter. The son had taken up brigandage. 'My lord,' said the porter, 'I always begged him not to go into politics.'

It was above all the miscellaneous character of politics which became unmistakable after these discussions. Politics was written, practised and theorised in a great variety of ways and there was often no connection between them. Lee Harvey Oswald and Hegel were both in one way or another engaged in politics: where did they touch? Without a clear focus on the genuine object of inquiry, studies of politics easily became incoherent. Sabine's famous history of political thought was accorded a certain perverse grandeur, but regarded as a scrapbook rather than a history. The older he got, the more Oakeshott tended to regard the very enterprise of a history of political thought as an impossible one.

It will be clear that some of this was pretty explosive stuff in the atmosphere of 1968-9, but the seminar flourished throughout this period, with the odd stand-off but no disruption. Bringing Vietnam or the capitalist system into these enquiries was soon universally recognised as a time-wasting solecism. In the early 1970s, the seminar was held in the East Building, and occasionally sounds of revolutionary revelry would float up from Houghton Street below, but the dialectic continued uninterrupted. Many people, including Oakeshott himself, smoked in those days, and it is somewhat embarrassing now to recall the blue haze which shrouded us all towards the end of the two hours.

Oakeshott in the mid-seventies was less imaginative than he had been, but he remained the star of the show. Students still treated the doctrine that there are different kinds of past as if they were responding to some kind of zen puzzle, like one hand clapping, but most of them absorbed the notion in the end. What never ceased to be a bone of contention was Oakeshott's unyielding defence of philosophy as having no practical implications. The idea that you cannot descend the ladder of theory offended every instinctive bone in their rationalist bodies; perhaps it suggested to them that studying philosophy was nothing but an irrelevant frivolity. But Oakeshott took Wittgenstein's view that philosophy leaves everything as it is. (He never met Wittgenstein, but once remarked, 'There were a lot of Viennese comedians around Cambridge in those days.') One seminar broke into a passionate discussion of what would follow if some cannibal tribal chief from a Pacific island read Kant's ethics and brought the categorical imperative to bear on the inherited customs of the tribe. For Oakeshott, the answer would depend on those people at that time, and any idea of the categorical imperative that touched practice would have entirely ceased to be a philosophical idea. Such a view denied the students the single manageable world in which they wanted to live. Oakeshott by contrast lived to the end in a plurality of worlds but, being a philosopher, never ceased to seek their coherence.

8

A Colleague's View

Elie Kedourie

I became familiar with Michael Oakeshott's name while still an undergraduate at LSE. It was probably in 1949 that I first came upon his introduction to Hobbes's *Leviathan*, read it and re-read it. Here was a writer, it then seemed to me, who approached political thought in a profound and subtle way – who did not look upon it as a storehouse from which to draw arguments in favour of this or that political position, or as a compendium of slogans which have somehow accumulated down the ages. For the undergraduate reader the introduction opened up vistas of profundity and subtlety which challenged him to respond with a deepening and refining of his own thought.

This text, however, remained a text – the glittering expression of a clearly exceptional mind. It stood as a monument calling upon you to comprehend its quality and power, but giving no clue, indeed providing no incentive, to discover what kind of man its author was.

It was during those same undergraduate years, 1949 and 1950, that I also came upon Oakeshott as editor of the *Cambridge Journal*. It was two articles published in there that made the man more accessible, that gave one the feeling that one could hold friendly converse, and perhaps tentatively explore possible affinities, with him. Curiously enough neither of the two articles was by Michael Oakeshott. One was by the economist S.R. Dennison and the other by C.H. Sisson. Dennison examined an attempt by an official working party (a title which I suppose indicated an aspiration to military despatch and efficiency) to establish how many nurses would be necessary two or three decades hence. Sisson explored, Conrad-like, the ambiguous world in which civil servants and politicians conducted their equivocal transactions. The textbooks at our disposal had, by contrast, assured us that economists and other social scientists could, with the utmost confidence, paint down to the smallest detail the lineaments of our future; and that the prime minister sat, primus inter pares, in the cabinet room, while secretaries, under-secretaries, assistant-secretaries and principals, like the members of an angelic hierarchy, transmitted, each in his turn, his wise and benevolent directions. Amid the intellectual dreariness of those post-war years to discover two such articles in one periodical gave one a thrill of intellectual liberation – an intellectual liberation for providing which the editor of the *Cambridge Journal* I felt to be above all responsible.

Though I did not then know Oakeshott personally, in 1951 and 1952 while I was still a graduate student I sent him two pieces which he accepted and published in the *Cambridge Journal*. The articles dealt with subjects with which he could not have been very familiar, but on the strength of what I sensed from the way he edited the *Journal* I felt that what I had to say might strike a responsive chord. And this is what I found when I came to know him as a colleague. His intellectual judgments were self-assured and acute. He found a way of going swiftly to the heart of the matter and seeing the essentials of an issue. It was this which until the end of his life gave an incomparable sparkle and charm to his mind, and which had the power to elicit in colleagues and friends during daily familiar intercourse an answering sparkle.

I became Michael's colleague in 1953, and it was my good fortune to remain one until his retirement. For most of these years he was the head of the Department of Government. The department was a large one, and grew larger during his tenure. All those years he despatched its affairs with efficiency, economy and elegance. He did this with seeming effortlessness. So much so that, to me at any rate, it looked as though the department ran itself.

8. A Colleague's View

When I retired at the end of the last session my colleagues gave me a dinner at which I quoted a passage from Macaulay's *History*, which I would like to reproduce here. Speaking of the character of the English Parliament, Macaulay said:

> To think nothing of symmetry and much of convenience; never to remove an anomaly merely because it is an anomaly; never to innovate except when some grievance is felt; never to innovate except so far as to get rid of the grievance; never to lay down any proposition of wider extent than the particular case for which it is necessary to provide; these are the rules which have from the age of John to the age of Victoria generally guided the deliberations of over two hundred and fifty Parliaments.

In quoting this passage I had above all in mind the spirit of Michael's administration of the Department of Government.

If prudence, and the eschewing of sudden administrative jars and revolutions, were the hallmarks of Michael's long tenure as head of the department, the case was quite otherwise with issues having to do with intellectual activity, the transmission of an intellectual tradition, and the criteria to be followed in determining the method and content of university teaching. Here, as I have said earlier, he was quick and decisive in establishing essentials and dismissing nonsense or flabbiness, however attractively or cunningly dressed up. I will end by illustrating this from his practice as a teacher.

In the nearly four decades of my life as a teacher at the School I have seen the academic board periodically seized with the desire to reform and improve the undergraduate degree, in response to some obscure but delusive urge to fashion a perfect, foolproof syllabus. One such convulsion gave Michael the opportunity to introduce his course on political thought, which became celebrated among the undergraduates. The course showed with what sureness of touch he married a commanding vision of the various styles of doing politics in the Western world, their vocabulary and idiom, with the requirements of an undergraduate audience, generally new to this kind of subject.

On another, later, occasion a fiat was handed down from Park Crescent, one of the first precursors of a deluge to come in succeeding years, that one-year graduate courses had to be instituted. The reasons were probably misconceived and banausic, and are now probably forgotten. Here too Michael seized the opportunity to establish a graduate course on the history of political thought. The course was genuinely a graduate course, in that it was not a simple extension of an undergraduate course but a philosophical enquiry into the organising ideas of any possible history of political thought. For this course he composed a series of papers which were read at a Tuesday afternoon seminar which, for those who took part in it, was a landmark in the teaching week. He continued to take the leading part in the seminar until 1980, long after his official retirement, and the papers he composed for it are now accessible in the volume *On History*, published in 1983 and dedicated to the seminar.

Goethe said that reading Kant was like entering a room filled with light. To those who were able to enjoy the sunlit and well-ordered domain of Michael's mind, the fortunate experience will remain with them, always.

9

In the Perspective of Western Thought

Noel O'Sullivan

Michael Oakeshott was best known during his lifetime for the most eloquent and profound philosophical defence of conservative politics that the present century has produced.

The core of that defence was not so much a doctrine, although many have tried to distil one out of his writings, as an intellectual and political style. While that style found many individual admirers, it was so uniquely Oakeshott's own that, in the nature of things, it could never become the basis for a school or movement of any kind. The uniqueness of Oakeshott's style does not, however, preclude an attempt to analyse briefly its three principal aspects.

The first aspect was Oakeshott's own temperament, the main feature of which was a love of freedom so radical and uncompromising that it imbued his conservatism with existentialist, and even anarchist, sympathies more akin to those of continental philosophers like Ortega y Gasset and Nicolai Berdyaev than to those of British conservatives like Burke. Needless to say, a conservatism of this kind could never become an establishment conservatism: it was always too philosophically exacting and too rigorously individualist in its political implications for the seal of conventionality to be placed upon it.

Taking a longer view, Oakeshott's temperament linked him closely to three thinkers whom he admired above all others: Montaigne, Cervantes, Pascal. With Montaigne he shared a feel for the human scale, refusing to indulge the traditional Western tendency to begin by assigning the human race a privileged place in the universe, only to end by complaining about the absurdity of a world which gives no sign of taking seriously that race's own exorbitant self-estimation. It is this modesty, this feel for the human scale, which accounts for the fact that Oakeshott's philosophy is free from the familiar expressions of alienation, absurdity, angst and nausea associated with contemporaries like Heidegger and Sartre. In contrast with theirs, his mood, like Montaigne's, was overwhelmingly positive, being characterised by composure, humour, gentleness and self-restraint.

With Montaigne he also shared a temperament notably free from any hint of censoriousness, and a rare capacity for friendship. It was in friendship, indeed, and what went with it – conversation – that Oakeshott found the supreme good. With Cervantes he shared his ultimate vision of the meaning of life: it is, he often remarked, an adventure. With Pascal, the first modern deconstructionist, Oakeshott shared a dislike of philosophic system-building. The approving remark he once made about another philosopher conveys not only the essence of his admiration for Pascal, but also his own conception of the limits of philosophy: 'His great achievement,' he said of John Locke, 'is to have thought systematically and to have escaped making a system.' The most timely expression of these sympathies, however, is to be found in the recently-published collection of Oakeshott's essays on the nature and purpose of education, *The Voice of Liberal Learning* (1989).

The second aspect of Oakeshott's style was a passion for limited government, more especially in the parliamentary form with which it has for centuries been associated in England. In *Rationalism in Politics* (1962), he identified the main enemy of limited government in our own age as ideological politics and state planning. Not surprisingly, his name was linked with other leading critics of collectivism such as von Mises, Hayek, Jewkes and Polanyi in a way which suggested that his main concern, like theirs, was the defence of capitalism. More recently, it was linked with such theorists of New Right philosophy as Robert Nozick, who equated limited with minimal government.

In 1975, however, Oakeshott's masterpiece, *On Human Conduct*, made amply clear that his central concern was not to defend capitalism, or the small state, or any of the other controversial objectives, such as élitism and an obscurantist concept of tradition, frequently ascribed to him. It was, rather, to re-establish contact between contemporary political theory and the classical ideal of civil association, in which he found the sole adequate foundation for limited politics. Oakeshott considered the key to the civil ideal – as developed by a long line of thinkers extending from Bodin and Hobbes, through Hegel, to John Stuart Mill – to be the concept of the state as a formal association of citizens united, not by a common purpose to be imposed by managerial government, but by mutual recognition of a civil authority which never constrains liberty because, unlike managerial government, it imposes no plan or purpose: what it does is to make laws which do not specify actions or purposes, but only lay down non-instrumental conditions to be observed by citizens in the course of pursuing whatever ends or purposes they may choose for themselves.

It is important to stress that Oakeshott never intended the ideal of civil association to provide a full account of the nature of the state. What he maintained was that only the ideal of civil association could provide a moral justification for the use of force by an association which men had not chosen to join. The ideal of civil association, in short, was intended only to provide a solution to the problem of legitimacy, as it had in earlier thinkers like Hobbes, and not to deny any managerial role at all to the state, as it has sometimes been assumed to do.

The third aspect of Oakeshott's style was a deeply sceptical conception of philosophy initially outlined in his first major work, *Experience and its Modes* (1933). Although the language in which he developed this philosophy drew heavily on the idealist tradition, the mood of disillusion which ran through that work reflected a standpoint that had neither the grandiose aspirations which inspired Hegel, nor the evangelical fervour which permeated English idealists like T.H. Green and Bosanquet. Philosophic scepticism reinforced a conservative disposition by restricting the philosopher to the modest task of identifying the presuppositions (or logical spectacles, so to speak) upon which all experience depends. Philosophy, that is to say, cannot help men to choose a way of life; it cannot propose solutions to conflicts between moral values or competing political systems; and it is unable to add any new facts to our knowledge of the world. All it can do is make us aware of the 'modality' or conditionality of all experience. The principal modes of experience Oakeshott identified as practice, history, science, and (in a later essay) aesthetics.

Both in *Experience and its Modes* and in a more recent book, *On History* (1983), some of his most original and brilliant work consisted in establishing that the only fully coherent mode of explanation available for the social sciences consists of historical explanation. So far as the status of philosophy itself is concerned, Oakeshott's scepticism was evident in his rejection of the claim, going back as far as Plato, that philosophy can provide an absolute standpoint from which to view experience.

More precisely, Oakeshott was prepared to admit that philosophic knowledge is in one sense absolute. What he rejected was the belief that it became absolute by virtue of performing the impossible task of enabling men to jump out of their skin, as it were, and occupy a position akin to God's. It is absolute only in the very modest sense of making us aware that our experience does in fact have presuppositions. It is by becoming reflexively aware of these presuppositions, in a word, and not by pursuing an ideal of objectivity which requires their elimination from experience, that we achieve the only feasible form of philosophic detachment.

Oakeshott was a fellow of Gonville and Caius College, Cambridge for 65 years. He was editor of the *Cambridge Journal*, in which he developed in the forties his polemic against the ethos of collectivism and ideological politics, which he called rationalist politics bearing no relation to the practice of politics. But he made his greatest public stamp when he took over from Harold Laski as Professor of Political Science at the London School of Economics in 1951.

The LSE had traditionally been associated with left-wing

9. In the Perspective of Western Thought

causes, and Oakeshott's arrival was a major innovation in the history of the school. He established an undergraduate course on political thought, running from Plato to John Stuart Mill, which became more or less the centre of gravity in that vast school. People from every manner of course went to his weekly lectures. A particular feature was the opening of the lecture. Other lecturers traditionally walked down the centre aisle of the theatre, but Oakeshott had found a mysterious back entrance that enabled him to appear through the curtain behind the lectern, greeted each time by a storm of applause. He also established in the 1960s a one-year masters degree devoted to historiography, the methodology of writing the history of philosophy. The masters course attracted students from all over the world and Oakeshott continued running it after he had retired from the LSE in 1969.

Those who attended his lectures and seminars will remember him as the least didactic of teachers. His manner always remained conversational and the least informed question by the most junior student was invariably treated with so much unaffected courtesy and attention that the student might be forgiven for feeling that no one had yet managed to formulate such an interesting thought so incisively. He was also the most accessible of dons, and would never leave department occasions arranged for students to meet and question their teachers informally until everyone who wished to speak to him had done so, no matter what the topic might be that concerned the students.

To ask what areas of Oakeshott's thought are most likely to prove of enduring significance is inevitably to end on a speculative note, but it may be hazarded that at least three major dimensions of his work are likely to prove of increasing relevance. At the most general level, Oakeshott's philosophy reveals how disillusion may become the basis of a positive, rather than a negative, view of life. A philosophy which contains that secret is what we need now more than any other. At a lower and more technical level, Oakeshott's analysis of the nature of historical enquiry is also likely to gain in relevance, as the last vestiges of the faith in positivism rapidly wane. Finally, so far as the political arena is concerned, his model of civil association is already beginning to be recognised as the greatest contribution to the restatement of liberal democratic theory made during the present century.

10

Bibliography

John Liddington

For drawing to my attention pieces by or about Michael Oakeshott, I am grateful to Lee Auspitz, V. Boyce, Professor Timothy Fuller, Dr R.A.D. Grant, Professor W.H. Greenleaf, Harold Hapke, Dr Ian Holliday, Nevil Johnson, Dr Tariq Modood, Oliver Starp, the late T.E. Utley, Dr Kevin Williams and Michael Oakeshott himself.

I. Published Work of Michael Oakeshott

This is a list of of Michael Oakeshott's published writings but generally omitting reprints. It incorporates Professor Greenleaf's bibliography in *Politics and Experience*, ed. P. King and B.C. Parekh (Cambridge: Cambridge University Press, 1968), pp. 409-17, to which I am greatly indebted. Items published before 1969 not included in Professor Greenleaf's compilation are marked with an asterisk [*].

1921

* 'Shylock the Jew', *Caian* (the magazine of Gonville and Caius College), 30: i (Michaelmas 1921), 61-7.

1922

* 'Lord Acton', *Caian*, 31: i (Michaelmas 1922), 14-23.

1926

Review of J. Needham (ed.), *Science, Religion and Reality*, in *Journal of Theological Studies*, 27 (1926), 317-19.

Review of A.C. Bouquet, *The Christian Religion and its Competitors Today*, in *Journal of Theological Studies*, 27 (1926), 440.

Review of E. Griffith-Jones, *Providence – Divine and Human*, in *Journal of Theological Studies*, 27 (1926), 440-1.

1927

Religion and the Moral Life (The 'D' Society Pamphlets, no. 2; Cambridge), pp. 13.
* 'In memoriam: Charles Montagu Doughty', *Caian*, 34: iii (Lent 1927), 117-33.
Review of T.Whittaker, *The Metaphysics of Evolution*, in *Cambridge Review*, 48 (1926-7), 230.
Review of R.B. Perry, *General Theory of Value*, in *Cambridge Review*, 48 (1926-7), 408.
Review of R.W. Sellars, *The Principles and Problems of Philosophy*, in *Cambridge Review*, 48 (1926-7), 429.
Review of F.J.E. Woodbridge, *The Realm of Mind*, in *Cambridge Review*, 49 (1927-8), 93.
Review of A.A. Jascalevich, *Three Conceptions of Mind*, in *Cambridge Review*, 49 (1927-8), 93.
Review of A.C. Widgery, *Contemporary Thought of Great Britain*, in *Cambridge Review*, 49 (1927-8), 156.
Review of C. Gore, *Can We then Believe?*, in *Journal of Theological Studies*, 28 (1927), 314-16.
Review of E.G. Selwyn (ed.), *Essays Catholic and Critical*, in *Journal of Theological Studies*, 28 (1927), 314-16.
Review of W.R. Bowie, *The Inescapable Christ*, in *Journal of Theological Studies*, 28 (1927), 314-16.
Review of P. Gardiner, *Modernism in the Church of England*, in *Journal of Theological Studies*, 28 (1927), 316.

1928

'The importance of the historical element in Christianity', *Modern Churchman*, 18 (1928-9), 360-71.

1929

* 'The authority of the state', *Modern Churchman*, 19 (1929-30), 313-27.
* Correspondence, *Modern Churchman*, 19 (1929-30), 614-15.
Review of J.S. Mackenzie, *Fundamental Problems of Life*, in *Journal of Philosophical Studies*, 4 (1929), 264-6.
Review of P.S. Belasco, *Authority in Church and State*, in *Journal of Theological Studies*, 30 (1929), 426-8.

1930

'The 55th Exhibition of the Cambridge Drawing Society', *Cambridge Review*, 51 (1929-30), 417.
Review of J. Marteau, *Clémenceau*, in *Cambridge Review*, 51 (1929-30), 332.
Review of J.C. Powys, *The Meaning of Culture*, in *Cambridge Review*, 51 (1929-30), 367-8.
Review of G.E.G. Catlin, *The Principles of Politics*, in *Cambridge Review*, 51 (1929-30), 400.
Review of K. Feiling, *What is Conservatism?*, in *Cambridge Review*, 51 (1929-30), 512.
Review of Ll. Powys, *The Pathetic Fallacy*, in *Cambridge Review*, 51 (1929-30), 512.
Review of H. Rashdall, *God and Man*, in *Cambridge Review*, 52 (1930-1), 39.
Review of G.G. Atkins, *The Making of the Christian Mind*, in *Journal of Theological Studies*, 31 (1930), 203-8.
Review of H.H. Farmer, *Experience of God*, in *Journal of Theological Studies*, 31 (1930), 302-3.

1931

'Scutari' (a poem), *Cambridge Review*, 53 (1931-2), 67.
Review of L.P. Smith, *Afterthoughts*, in *Cambridge Review*, 52 (1930-1), 287.
Review of F.H. Bradley, *Aphorisms*, in *Cambridge Review*, 52 (1930-1), 287.
Review of L. Britton, *Love and Hunger*, in *Cambridge Review*, 52 (1930-1), 351.
Review of J.B. Pratt, *Adventures in Philosophy and Religion*, in *Cambridge Review*, 52 (1930-1), 511.
Review of H. Driesch, *Ethical Principles in Theory and Practice*, in *Journal of Theological Studies*, 32 (1931), 326-7.
Review of F.J. Sheen, *Religion without God*, in *Journal of Theological Studies*, 32 (1931), 434-5.
Review of K. Heim, *The New Divine Order*, in *Journal of Theological Studies*, 32 (1931), 434-5.
Review of E. Holmes, *Philosophy without Metaphysics*, in *Journal of Theological Studies*, 32 (1931), 434-5.

1932

'Cracow' (a poem), *Cambridge Review*, 53 (1931-2), 266.
'John Locke', *Cambridge Review*, 54 (1932-3), 72-3.
'The new Bentham', *Scrutiny*, 1 (1932-3), 114-31.
Review of F.J.C. Hearnshaw (ed.), *Political and Social Ideas of the Age*

of *Reaction and Reconstruction*, in *Cambridge Review*, 53 (1931-2), 332.

1933

Experience and its Modes (Cambridge: Cambridge University Press), pp. vii + 358.
Review of M. Ruthnaswamy, *The State*, in *Cambridge Review*, 54 (1932-3), 359.
Review of J. Macmurray, *Interpreting the Universe*, in *Cambridge Review*, 54 (1932-3), 395.
Review of C.R. Morris, *Idealistic Logic*, in *Cambridge Review*, 55 (1933-4), 152.
* Review of L. Chestov, *In Jacob's Balance*, in *Scrutiny*, 2 (1933-4), 101-4.

1934

* 'Edward Bullough' (obituary), *Caian*, 43: i (Michaelmas 1934), 1-11.
Review of M. Grant, *A New Argument for God's Survival*, in *Cambridge Review*, 55 (1933-4), 332.
Review of L. Curtis, *Civitas Dei*, in *Cambridge Review*, 55 (1933-4), 450.
Review of O. Gierke, *Natural Law and the Theory of Society, 1500 to 1800* (tr. Barker), in *Cambridge Review*, 56 (1934-5), 11-12.
Review of H. Levy and others, *Aspects of Dialectical Materialism*, in *Cambridge Review*, 56 (1934-5), 108-9.
Review of A.N. Whitehead, *Adventures of Ideas*, in *Journal of Theological Studies*, 35 (1934), 73-5.
Review of C.D. Burns, *The Horizon of Experience*, in *Journal of Theological Studies*, 35 (1934), 75-6.
Review of G. Michaelis, *Richard Hooker als Politischer Denker*, in *Journal of Theological Studies*, 35 (1934), 76.

1935

* 'R.A.S. Macfie' (obituary), *Caian*, 44: i (Michaelmas 1935), 41-2.
'Thomas Hobbes', *Scrutiny*, 4 (1935-6), 263-77.
Review of H.G. Wood, *Christianity and the Nature of History*, in *Cambridge Review*, 56 (1934-5), 248.
Review of E.F. Carritt, *Morals and Politics*, in *Cambridge Review*, 56 (1934-5), 449.
Review of M.B. Foster, *The Political Philosophies of Plato and Hegel*, in *Cambridge Review*, 57 (1935-6), 74.
Review of W. Tilly, *Right: a Study in Physical and Moral Order*, in *Journal of Theological Studies*, 36 (1935), 322-3.
Review of H.G. Wood, *Christianity and the Nature of History*, in *Journal of Theological Studies*, 36 (1935), 323-4.

Bibliography

Review of J.C. McKerrow, *Religion and History*, in *Journal of Theological Studies*, 36 (1935), 323-4.

1936

(With G.T. Griffith), *A Guide to the Classics, or, How to Pick the Derby Winner* (London: Faber and Faber), pp. 136.

'History and the social sciences', in the Institute of Sociology, *The Social Sciences* (London: Le Play House Press), pp. 71-81.

'The servant girl who burnt Carlyle's MS', *Listener*, 15 (1936), 459-60. Reprinted in A. Bryant and others, *Imaginary Biographies* (London: Allen and Unwin, 1936), pp. 61-72.

'Robert Jenkins', in A. Bryant and others, *op. cit.*, pp. 73-81.

Review of W. Brock, *An Introduction to Contemporary German Philosophy*, in *Cambridge Review*, 57 (1935-6), 195.

* Review of N. Berdyaev, *The Meaning of History*, in *Cambridge Review*, 57 (1935-6), 453.

Review of L. Strauss, *The Political Philosophy of Hobbes*, in *Cambridge Review*, 58 (1936-7), 150.

* Review of C.C.J. Webb, *The Historical Element in Religion*, in *Journal of Theological Studies*, 37 (1936), 96-8.

Review of F.H. Bradley, *Collected Essays*, in *Philosophy*, 11 (1936), 114-16.

Review of B. Pfannenstill, *Bernard Bosanquet's Philosophy of the State*, in *Philosophy*, 11 (1936), 482-3.

1937

'Dr. Leo Strauss on Hobbes', *Politica*, 2 (1936-7), 364-79.

Review of K. Mannheim, *Ideology and Utopia*, in *Cambridge Review*, 58 (1936-7), 257.

Review of F. Birch, *This Freedom of Ours*, in *Cambridge Review*, 59 (1937-8), 55.

Review of L. Strauss, *The Political Philosophy of Hobbes*, in *Philosophy*, 12 (1937), 239-41.

Review of M. Roberts, *The Modern Mind*, in *Scrutiny*, 6 (1937-8), 208-10.

1938

'The concept of a philosophical jurisprudence', *Politica*, 3 (1938), 203-22, 345-60.

Review of R.G. Collingwood, *The Principles of Art*, in *Cambridge Review*, 59 (1937-8), 487.

1939

The Social and Political Doctrines of Contemporary Europe (Cambridge: Cambridge University Press), pp. xxiii + 224.
The same, with additions and corrections, pp. xxiii + 241.
'The claims of politics', *Scrutiny*, 8 (1939-40), 146-51.
'Geoffrey Rossetti' (obituary), *Cambridge Review*, 60 (1938-9), 166-7.
Review of J. Marshall, *Swords and Symbols*, in *Philosophy*, 14 (1939), 493-4.
* Review of K.B. Smellie, *Reason in Politics*, in *Politica*, 4 (1939), 167-8.

1940

Review of E.F.M. Durbin, *The Politics of Democratic Socialism*, in *Cambridge Review*, 61 (1939-40), 347, 348 and 350.

1941

The Social and Political Doctrines of Contemporary Europe, 2nd edition (Cambridge: Cambridge University Press), pp. xxiii + 241.
Review of G. Wallas, *Men and Ideas*, in *Philosophy*, 16 (1941), 95.

1942

The Social and Political Doctrines of Contemporary Europe, with five additional prefaces by F.A. Ogg (Cambridge: Cambridge University Press; New York: Macmillan), pp. xxiii + 241.

1946

Hobbes's *Leviathan* (edited with an introduction; Oxford: Blackwell), pp. lxvii + 468.
Review of B. Croce, *Politics and Morals*, in *Philosophy*, 21 (1946), 184.

1947

(With G.T. Griffith), *A New Guide to the Derby: How to Pick the Winner* (London: Faber and Faber), pp. 133.
'Rationalism in politics', *Cambridge Journal*, 1 (1947-8), 81-98, 145-57.
'The "collective dream of civilisation"', *Listener*, 37 (1947), 966-7.
Review of R.G. Collingwood, *The Idea of History*, in *English Historical Review*, 62 (1947), 84-6.
* Review of W.A. Orton, *The Liberal Tradition*, in *English Historical Review*, 62 (1947), 262.

Review of J. Bowle, *Western Political Thought*, in *Spectator*, 179 (1947), 626.

1948

'Scientific politics', *Cambridge Journal*, 1 (1947-8), 347-58.
'Contemporary British politics', *Cambridge Journal*, 1 (1947-8), 474-90.
'Science and society', *Cambridge Journal*, 1 (1947-8), 689-97.
'The Tower of Babel', *Cambridge Journal*, 2 (1948-9), 67-83.
Review of H.D. Lasswell, *The Analysis of Political Behaviour*, in *Cambridge Journal*, 1 (1947-8), 326, 328.
Review of L. Whistler, *The English Festivals*, in *Cambridge Journal*, 1 (1947-8), 382, 384.
Review of J. Lavrin, *Nietzsche*, in *Cambridge Journal*, 1 (1947-8), 450, 452.
Review of W.T. Jones (ed.), *Masters of Political Thought* (vol. 2), in *Cambridge Journal*, 1 (1947-8), 636-7.
Review of K.B. Smellie, *Why We Read History*, in *Cambridge Journal*, 1 (1947-8), 766-7.
Review of S. Campion, *Father, a Portrait of G.C. Coulton*, in *Cambridge Journal*, 2 (1948-9), 116, 118.
Review of the Earl of Lytton, *Bulwer-Lytton*, in *Cambridge Journal*, 2 (1948-9), 188.
* Review of G. Bryson, *Man and Society: the Scottish Inquiry of the Eighteenth Century*, in *English Historical Review*, 63 (1948), 272-3.
* Review of M. Ginsberg, *Reason and Unreason in Society*, in *English Historical Review*, 63 (1948), 414-15.
Review of R B. Perry, *Puritanism and Democracy*, in *Philosophy*, 23 (1948), 86-7.
Review of C.E.M. Joad, *Decadence*, in *Spectator*, 180 (1948), 290, 292.

1949

'The political economy of freedom', *Cambridge Journal*, 2 (1948-9), 212-29.
'The universities', *Cambridge Journal*, 2 (1948-9), 515-42.
'J.D. Mabbott: *The State and the Citizen*', *Mind*, 58 (1949), 378-89.
Review of F. Williams, *The Triple Challenge*, in *Cambridge Journal*, 2 (1948-9), 313-14.
Review of J.D. Mabbott, *The State and the Citizen*, in *Cambridge Journal*, 2 (1948-9), 316, 318.
Review of F. Sternberg, *How to Stop the Russians Without War*, in *Cambridge Journal*, 2 (1948-9), 435-7.
Review of G.C. Field, *Principles and Ideals in Politics*, in *Cambridge Journal*, 2 (1948-9), 444, 446.
Review of Sir E.W. Whittaker, *The Modern Approach to Descartes'*

Problem, in *Cambridge Journal*, 2 (1948-9), 629-30.
Review of S.M. Jacobs, *Notes on Descartes' Règles*, in *Cambridge Journal*, 2 (1948-9), 629-30.
Review of P. Valéry, *Descartes*, in *Cambridge Journal*, 2 (1948-9), 629-30.
Review of H. Selsam, *Socialism and Ethics*, in *Cambridge Journal*, 2 (1948-9), 692-4.
Review of E. Dudley, *The Tree of Commonwealth* (ed. Brodie), in *Cambridge Journal*, 2 (1948-9), 763-4.
Review of A. Koestler, *Insight and Outlook*, in *Spectator*, 183 (1949), 20, 22.
* Review of H. Butterfield, *The Origins of Modern Science, 1300-1800*, in *Times Literary Supplement*, (25 November, 1949), 761-3.

1950

'Rational conduct', *Cambridge Journal*, 4 (1950-1), 3-27.
* 'Stalin's four weak points', *Evening Standard*, (20 November, 1950), 9.
'The idea of a university', *Listener*, 43 (1950), 424-6.
* Correspondence, *Times Literary Supplement*, (4 August, 1950), 485.
Review of J. W. Watmough, *Cambridge Conversations*, in *Cambridge Journal*, 3 (1949-50), 252-4.
Review of J. Plamenatz, *The English Utilitarians*, in *Cambridge Journal*, 3 (1949-50), 312-13.
Review of Sir R. Filmer, *Patriarcha and other Political Works* (ed. Laslett), in *Cambridge Journal*, 3 (1949-50), 384.
* Review of J.W. Gough, *John Locke's Political Philosophy*, in *English Historical Review*, 65 (1950), 550.
Review of Sir R. Filmer, *Patriarcha and other Political Works* (ed. Laslett), in *Philosophy*, 25 (1950), 280-1.
Review of G. Ryle, *The Concept of Mind*, in *Spectator*, 184 (1950), 20, 22.
Review of J. Godley, *Tell Me the Next One*, in *Spectator*, 184 (1950), 734.

1951

Political Education (Cambridge: Bowes and Bowes), pp. 28.
'Mr. Carr's first volume', *Cambridge Journal*, 4 (1950-1), 344-52.
'The B.B.C.', *Cambridge Journal*, 4 (1950-1), 543-54.
'A reminder from "Leviathan"', *Observer*, (29 July, 1951), 4.
* Correspondence, *New Statesman and Nation*, 42 (28 July, 1951), 100.
Review of T. Wilson, *Modern Capitalism and Economic Progress*, in *Cambridge Journal*, 4 (1950-1), 504-6.
Review of J.H.S. Burleigh, *The City of God*, in *Cambridge Journal*, 4 (1950-1), 567-8, 570, 572.
Review of R.H. Barrow, *Introduction to St. Augustine*, in *Cambridge Journal*, 4 (1950-1), 567-8, 570, 572.

Bibliography

Review of T.H. Marshall, *Citizenship and Social Class*, in *Cambridge Journal*, 4 (1950-1), 629-30.
Review of N. Machiavelli, *The Discourses* (ed. Walker), in *Cambridge Journal*, 4 (1950-1), 698.
Review of G.J. Renier, *History, its Purpose and Method*, in *Philosophical Quarterly*, 1 (1950-1), 284-5.
Review of C. Morgan, *Liberties of the Mind*, in *Spectator*, 186 (1951), 419.
Review of G. Santayana, *Dominations and Powers*, in *Spectator*, 187 (1951), 578.
* Review of D.W. Brogan, *The Price of Revolution*, in *Spectator*, 187 (1951), 825.
* Review of J. Bowle, *Hobbes and his Critics*, in *Time and Tide*, 32 (1951), 977-8.

1952

Review of E.M. Forster, *Two Cheers for Democracy*, in *Cambridge Journal*, 5 (1951-2), 436-8.
* Review of B. de Jouvenel, *The Ethics of Redistribution*, in *Clare Market Review* (London School of Economics), 47: ii (Lent 1952), 4-5.
Review of W.H. Walsh, *An Introduction to Philosophy of History*, in *Philosophical Quarterly*, 2 (1952), 276-7.
Review of E. von Kuehnelt-Leddihn, *Liberty or Equality*, in *Spectator*, 188 (1952), 338, 340.
Review of Lord Radcliffe, *The Problem of Power*, in *Spectator*, 188 (1952), 451-2.

1953

Review of D. Forbes, *The Liberal Anglican Idea of History*, in *Cambridge Journal*, 4 (1952-3), 248-51.
Review of M. Cranston, *Freedom*, in *Spectator*, 190 (1953), 579.
Review of T.D. Weldon, *The Vocabulary of Politics*, in *Spectator*, 191 (1953), 405-6.

1954

Review of A. Dru (ed.), *The Letters of Jacob Burckhardt*, in *Encounter*, 2: vi (1954), 69-70, 72-4.
Review of H. Read, *Anarchy and Order*, in *Spectator*, 192 (1954), 593-4.
Review of J. Bowle, *Politics and Opinion in the Nineteenth Century*, in *Spectator*, 193 (1954), 66, 69.
Review of M. Duverger, *Political Parties*, in *Spectator*, 193 (1954), 92-3.

Review of R. Kirk, *The Conservative Mind*, in *Spectator*, 193 (1954), 472, 474.
Review of E. Benes, *Memoirs*, in *Spectator*, 193 (1954), 639-40.

1955

La Idea de Gobierno en la Europa Moderna (Madrid: Ateneo), pp. 33.
'The customer is never wrong', *Listener*, 54 (1955), 301-2.
Review of H. Marcuse, *Reason and Revolution*, in *Spectator*, 194 (1955), 404-5.
Review of K.C. Wheare, *Government by Committee*, in *Spectator*, 195 (1955), 129.
Review of H. Butterfield, *Man on his Past*, in *Spectator*, 195 (1955), 595-6.
Review of P. Bloomfield, *Uncommon People*, in *Spectator*, 195 (1955), 871-2.

1956

Political Education [reprinted with some minor alterations and additions in P.J. Laslett (ed.), *Philosophy, Politics and Society*, 1st series (Oxford: Blackwell), pp. 1-21].
Review of G. Barraclough, *History in a Changing World*, in *Spectator*, 196 (1956), 220-1.
Review of C. Rossiter, *Conservatism in America*, in *Spectator*, 196 (1956), 451-2.
Review of A.J. Ayer and others, *Studies in Communication*, in *Spectator*, 196 (1956), 502.
Review of J. Bowle, *Minos or Minotaur?*, in *Spectator*, 197 (1956), 31-2.
Review of G. Salvemini, *Mazzini*, in *Spectator*, 197 (1956), 459-60.
Review of J. Brooke, *The Chatham Administration*, in *Spectator*, 197 (1956), 746.

1957

'Die Massen in der repräsentativen Demokratie', in A. Hunold (ed.), *Masse und Demokratie* (Erlenbach-Zürich und Stuttgart: Rentsch), pp. 189-214.
Review of B. de Jouvenel, *Sovereignty*, in *Crossbow*, 1 (1957), 43-4.
Review of Lady Stenton, *The Englishwoman in History*, in *Spectator*, 198 (1957), 459-60.
Review of H. Warrender, *The Political Philosophy of Thomas Hobbes*, in *Spectator*, 199 (1957), 198.
Review of G. Heckscher, *The Study of Comparative Government and Politics*, in *Spectator*, 199 (1957), 490-1.
Review of J. Lewis, *Marxism and the Open Mind*, in *Spectator*, 199 (1957), 654.

Bibliography

Review of H. Butterfield, *George III and the Historians*, in *Spectator*, 199 (1957), 718.

1958

'The activity of being an historian', *Historical Studies* I, ed. T.D. Williams (London: Bowes and Bowes), pp. 1-19.
* Review of T.E. Utley and J.S. Maclure, *Documents of Modern Political Thought*, in *Crossbow*, 1 (1958), 42-3.
Review of M. Polanyi, *Personal Knowledge*, in *Encounter*, 9: iii (1958), 77-80.

1959

The Voice of Poetry in the Conversation of Mankind (London: Bowes and Bowes), pp. 63.
'Nazism', in *Chambers Encyclopaedia*, 9, pp. 737-9.

1961

'The masses in representative democracy', in A. Hunold (ed.), *Freedom and Serfdom: an Anthology of Western Thought* (Dordrecht, Holland: Reidel), pp. 151-70.
Review of J. Chiari, *Realism and Imagination*, in *British Journal of Aesthetics*, 1 (1960-1), 198-9.
* Review of H.J. Blackham, *Political Discipline in a Free Society*, in *Sunday Telegraph*, (26 March, 1961).
* Review of M. Cole, *The Story of Fabian Socialism*, in *Sunday Telegraph*, (5 November, 1961).

1962

Rationalism in Politics and Other Essays (London: Methuen; New York: Barnes & Noble Books), pp. 333. This comprises the following essays, of which seven were previously published, some in a slightly different form: 'Rationalism in politics' (1947); 'The political economy of freedom' (1949); 'The Tower of Babel' (1948); 'Rational conduct' (1950); 'Political education' (1951); 'The activity of being an historian' (1955); 'On being conservative' (1956); 'The voice of poetry in the conversation of mankind' (1959); 'The moral life in the writings of Thomas Hobbes' (1960); 'The study of politics in a university' (1961).
Hobbes's *Leviathan*, ed. M. Oakeshott with an introduction by R.S. Peters (New York: Collier Books), pp. 511.
* Correspondence, *Times Literary Supplement*, (12 October, 1962), 793.
Review of P. Laslett (ed.), *Locke's Two Treatises of Government*, in *Historical Journal*, 5 (1962), 97-100.

Review of R. Shackleton, *Montesquieu: a Critical Biography*, in *Modern Language Review*, 57 (1962), 442-4.
Review of H. Arendt, *Between Past and Future*, in *Political Science Quarterly*, 77 (1962), 88-90.

1964

'Political laws and captive audiences', in G.R. Urban (ed.), *Talking to Eastern Europe* (London: Eyre and Spottiswoode), pp. 291-301.
R. Bassett, *The Essentials of Parliamentary Democracy*, 2nd ed.; edited with an introduction (London: Cass), pp. xxiv + 214.

1965

'Rationalism in politics: a reply to Professor Raphael', *Political Studies*, 13 (1965), 89-92.
* Review of D. Kelly, *The Hungry Sheep*, in *Daily Telegraph*, (2 September, 1965).
Review of The Bow Group, *The Conservative Opportunity*, in *New Society*, 6 (1965), 26-7.
Review of P. Laslett and W.G. Runciman (eds.), *Philosophy, Politics and Society* (2nd series), in *Philosophical Quarterly*, 15 (1965), 281-2.

1966

Rationalismus in der Politik (Neuwied und Berlin: Luchterhard).
Review of J.C. Holt, *Magna Carta*, in *Government and Opposition*, 1 (1965-6), 266-71.
Review of J. Lively (ed.), *The Works of Joseph de Maistre*, in *New Society*, 7 (10 February, 1966), 28-9.
* Review of D.P. Calleo, *Coleridge and the Idea of the Modern State*, in *New Society*, 7 (9 June, 1966), 28-9.

1967

'Learning and teaching', in R.S. Peters (ed.), *The Concept of Education* (London: Routledge and Kegan Paul), pp. 156-76.
* 'Personal retrospect: by a scholar', in *St. George's School, Harpenden (1907 – 1967): a Portrait of the Founders*, compiled H.W. Howe (Harpenden: St. George's School), pp. 14-18.
* 'The definition of a university', *Journal of Educational Thought*, 1 (1967), 129-42.
* 'Nazism', in *Chambers Encyclopaedia* (new rev. ed.), 11, pp. 722-4.
Review of K. Brown (ed.), *Hobbes Studies*, in *English Historical Review*, 82 (1967), 123-5.

Review of J.R. Lucas, *The Principles of Politics*, in *Political Studies*, 15 (1967), 224-7.

1968

Review of F.H. Hinsley, *Sovereignty*, in *English Historical Review*, 83 (1968), 441-2.

1971

'Education: the engagement and its frustration', *Proceedings of the Annual Conference: Philosophy of Education Society of Great Britain*, 5 (January 1971), 19-49.
Review of D. Thomson, *The Aims of History*, in *English Historical Review*, 86 (1971), 597.
Review of K. Marx, *Critique of Hegel's Philosophy of Right* (ed. O'Malley), in *Spectator*, 226 (1971), 192-3.

1972

'Education: the engagement and its frustration', in *Education and the Development of Reason*, ed. R.F. Dearden, P.H. Hirst and R.S. Peters (London: Routledge and Kegan Paul), pp. 19-49.
Untitled paragraph, in London School of Economics, *Library Appeal*.

1974

Review of T.A. Spragens, Jr. *The Politics of Motion: the World of Thomas Hobbes*, in *Government and Opposition*, 9 (1974), 237-44.

1975

Hobbes on Civil Association (Oxford: Basil Blackwell), pp. vi + 154. This comprises the following essays, all previously published, the first in a somewhat different form: 'Introduction to *Leviathan*' (1946); 'The moral life in the writings of Thomas Hobbes' (1960); 'Dr. Leo Strauss on Hobbes' (1937); 'Leviathan: a myth' (1947: 'The "collective dream of civilisation" ').
On Human Conduct (Oxford: Oxford University Press), pp. viii + 329.
'A place of learning', *Colorado College Studies*, 12 (January 1975), 6-29.
'Talking politics', *National Review*, 27 (1975), 1345-7, 1423-8.
'The vocabulary of a modern European state', *Political Studies*, 23 (1975), 319-41, 409-14.
Review of S. Avineri, *Hegel's Theory of the Modern State*, in *European Studies Review*, 5 (1975), 217-20.

1976

'On misunderstanding human conduct: a reply to my critics', *Political Theory*, 4 (1976), 353-67.

1978

Review of *Conservative Essays* (ed. Cowling), in *Daily Telegraph*, (29 June, 1978).
Review of N. Johnson, *In Search of the Constitution*, in *Public Administration*, 56 (1978), 102-5.

1980

'Preface' to *The Form of Ideology* (ed. Manning) (London: George Allen and Unwin, 1980) pp. vii-viii.
Review of Q. Skinner, *The Foundations of Modern Political Thought*, in *Historical Journal*, 23 (1980), 449-53.

1983

On History and Other Essays (Oxford: Basil Blackwell), pp. 198. This comprises the following essays, none previously published: Three essays on history; 'I Present, future and past'; 'II Historical events: The fortuitous, the causal, the similar, the correlative, the analogous, and the contingent'; 'III Historical Change: identity and continuity'; 'The rule of law'; 'The Tower of Babel'.
'This towering folly', *Times*, (26 February, 1983), 10 [excerpt from 'The Tower of Babel', in *On History and Other Essays*].

1985

La Condotta Umana (Bologna: Società Editrice Il Mulino SPA).

1988

Review of *Conservative Thoughts: Essays from The Salisbury Review* (ed. Scruton), in *Spectator*, 261 (9 July, 1988), 60.
Review of *Conservative Thinkers: Essays from The Salisbury Review* (ed. Scruton), in *Spectator*, 261 (9 July, 1988), 60.

1989

The Voice of Liberal Learning: Michael Oakeshott on Education (ed. T. Fuller) (New Haven and London: Yale University Press), pp. 166. This comprises the following essays, all previously published: 'A place of learning' (1975); 'Learning and teaching' (1967);

'Education: the engagement and its frustration' (1972); 'The idea of a university' (1950); 'The universities' (1949); 'Political education' (1951 and 1962).

1991

Rationalism in Politics and Other Essays (new and expanded edition; ed. T. Fuller) (Indianapolis: Liberty Press), pp. xxvi + 556. This comprises the essays in the 1962 edition of *Rationalism in Politics* and the following essays, all, other than 'Political discourse', previously published: 'Political discourse'; 'The new Bentham' (1932); 'Introduction to Leviathan' (1946 and 1974); 'Logos and telos' (1974: review of T.A. Spragens, Jr. *The Politics of Motion: the World of Thomas Hobbes*); 'The masses in representative democracy' (1961); 'Talking politics' (1975).

II. Published Work on Oakeshott

A. Reviews

Reviews of 'Experience and its Modes' (1933)

Anon *London Quarterly and Holborn Review*, 159 (1934), 279.
—— *Psychological Medicine*, 9 (1979), 602-3.
—— *Times Literary Supplement*, (26 April, 1934), 294.
J.R. Balow *Australian Journal of Politics and History*, 25 (1979), 289-90.
W.G. de Burgh *Hibbert Journal*, 33 (1934), 144-50.
R.G. Collingwood *Cambridge Review*, 55 (1933-4), 249-50.
I. Crowther *Salisbury Review*, 5 (April 1987), 71.
T.E. Jessop *Philosophy*, 11 (1936), 357-9.
T.M. Knox *Oxford Magazine*, 52 (1934), 551-2.
S.P. Lamprecht *Journal of Philosophy*, 31 (1934), 163-4.
J. Oman *Journal of Theological Studies*, 35 (1934), 314-16.
L.R. Perry *British Journal of Educational Studies*, 16 (1968), 96-7.
L.S. Stebbing *Mind*, 43 (1934), 403-5.
A. Sullivan *New Republic*, 195 (22 December, 1986), 28-34, 36.

Reviews of 'The Social and Political Doctrines of Contemporary Europe' (1939)

Anon *Times Literary Supplement*, (1 April, 1939), 182.
W.G. de Burgh *Mind*, 49 (1940), 100-2.
S.J.G. *Dublin Review*, 205 (1939), 195-7.
J.L. Hammond *Manchester Guardian*, (25 April, 1939), 7.
J.G. Kerwin *Commonweal*, 30 (1939), 191.
—— *Journal of Political Economy*, 51 (1943), 278-9.

H. Kohn *The Nation* (New York), 149 (1939), 299-300.
H.D. Lasswell *Annals of the American Academy of Political and Social Science*, 229 (September 1943), 193.
E.J. Passant *Philosophy*, 14 (1939), 373-4.
J.S. Roucek *American Sociological Review*, 4 (1939), 737-8.
—— *Annals of the American Academy of Political and Social Science*, 204 (July 1939), 187-8.
G. de Ruggiero *Politica*, 4 (1939), 284-5.
W. Sandelius *American Political Science Review*, 33 (1939), 932-3.
M.Q. Sibley *American Political Science Review*, 33 (1943), 183.

lf15022reviews of Hobbes's 'Leviathan' (1946)

Anon *Times Literary Supplement*, (11 January, 1947) 19.
C. Read *William & Mary Quarterly*, 3rd series, 5 (1948), 409-12.
K. Schilling *Zeitschrift für Philosophische Forschung*, 1 (1947), 193-4.

Reviews of 'A New Guide to the Derby: How to Pick the Winner' (1947)

Anon *Times Literary Supplement*, (24 May, 1947), 259.

Reviews of 'Political Education' (1951)

Anon *Times Literary Supplement*, (1 June, 1951), 341 (editorial).
R.H.S. Crossman *New Statesman and Nation*, 42 (1951), 60-1.
P. Laslett *Cambridge Journal*, 5 (1951-2), 765-6, 768.
W.J.M. Mackenzie *Universities Quarterly*, 9 (1955), 351-63. ('Political theory and political education').
J.C. Rees *Mind*, 62 (1953), 68-74 ('Professor Oakeshott on political education').

Reviews of 'The Voice of Poetry in the Conversation of Mankind' (1959)

Anon *Times Literary Supplement*, (11 December, 1959) 725 (editorial).
L. Clark *Time and Tide*, 41 (1960), 62.
A.R. Fell *Queen's Quarterly*, 67 (1960-1), 698-9.
G. Johnson *Poetry Review*, 51 (1960), 43.
R. Lawrence *English*, 13 (1960-1), 29-31.
C. Madge *Modern Language Review*, 55 (1960), 622-3.
V. Minogue *Twentieth Century* (London), 167 (1960), 226-34 ('Philosopher go home! poetry and Professor Oakeshott').
B.E. Owen *Contemporary Review*, 198 (1960), 519-20.
L.R. Perry *New Era in Home and School*, 41 (1960), 62-4.
R. Wollheim *Spectator*, 203 (1959), 881.

Reviews of 'Rationalism in Politics and Other Essays' (1962)

Anon *Christian Century*, 79 (1962), 1328.
—— *Hibbert Journal*, 61 (1962-3), 100, 102.
—— *International Relations* (London), 2:vi (October 1962), 405.
—— *Times*, (13 September, 1962), 11.
—— *Times Literary Supplement*, (28 September, 1962), 753-4.
H. Bernard-Maitre *Erasmus* (Wiesbaden), 17 (1965), 406-7.
W. Berns *American Political Science Review*, 57 (1963), 670-1.
J. Bowle *Daily Telegraph*, (2 November, 1962).
G.E.G. Catlin *Western Political Quarterly*, 16 (1963), 259-61.
G.C. Duncan *Australasian Journal of Philosophy*, 41 (1963), 112-20.
D. Emmet *Philosophical Quarterly*, 13 (1963), 283-4.
H. Fairlie *Spectator*, 209 (1962), 644-5.
C. Falck *New Left Review*, 18: i (January-February 1963), 60-71 ('Romanticism in politics').
J.H. Franklin *Journal of Philosophy*, 60 (1963), 811-20.
O. Gass *New Republic*, 2516: vi (9 February, 1963), 21-6 ('Politics of dead center').
C.J. Hughes *Philosophical Books*, 4: i (1963), 25-6.
H.V. Jaffa *National Review*, (22 October, 1963), 360-2.
D. Kettler *World Politics*, 16 (1964), 483-9 ('The cheerful discourses of Michael Oakeshott').
R. Kirk *Annals of the American Academy of Political and Social Science*, 347 (May 1963), 181.
A. Kolnai *Philosophy*, 40 (1965), 68-71.
H. Kuhn *Zeitschrift für Politik*, 10 (1963), 194-7.
P. Laslett *Manchester Guardian*, (14 September, 1962), 4.
G. Lavau *Revue Française de Science Politique*, 14 (1964), 124-6.
G. Lichtheim *Commentary*, 35 (1963), 168-72 ('A settled habit of behaviour').
J.D. Mabbott *Mind*, 72 (1963), 609-11.
W.J.M. Mackenzie *Universities Quarterly*, 17 (1962-3), 81-3.
D. Marquand *New Statesman and Nation*, 64 (1962), 574.
B. Miller *Listener*, 68 (1962), 424-5.
B. de Mott *Harper's Magazine* (New York), (March 1963), 106, 108, 110.
P.H. Partridge *Australian Journal of Politics and History*, 9 (1963), 109-13 ('The study of politics').
J. Plamenatz *British Journal of Sociology*, 14 (1963), 284-6.
D.D. Raphael *Political Studies*, 12 (1964), 202-15. See also M. Oakeshott, 'Rationalism in Politics: a reply to Professor Raphael', *Political Studies*, 13 (1965), 89-92; and D.D. Raphael, 'Rationalism in Politics: a note on Professor Oakeshott's reply', *Political Studies*, 13 (1965), 395-7.
P. Schwartz *Clare Market Review*, 57: ii (Winter 1962), 60-3.
V. Weiss *Philosophisches Jahrbuch*, 85 (1978), 167.

F.G. Wilson *Universities Bookman*, 4 (Autumn 1963), 19-23 ('Oakeshott and conservatism').

Reviews of 'Hobbes on Civil Association' (1975)

L.H.C. *Heythrop Journal*, 23 (1982), 105.
J. Lively *Times Higher Education Supplement*, (13 February, 1976), 20.
K.R. Minogue *Political Studies*, 24 (1976), 212-13.
D.E.B. Pollard *Philosophical Studies* (Dublin), 24 (1976), 314-15.
A. Seller *Philosophical Books*, 17 (1976), 54-7.
T.A. Spragens, Jr. *American Political Science Review*, 72 (1978), 652-3.
L.J. Thro *Modern Schoolman*, 56 (1977), 289-92.
C. Walton *Journal of the History of Philosophy*, 14 (1976), 499.

Reviews of 'On Human Conduct' (1975)

F.J. Abbate *Metaphilosophy*, 9 (1978), 175-80.
J.E.J. Altham *Cambridge Review*, 97 (24 October, 1975), 23-5.
Anon *British Book News*, (July 1975).
—— *Economist*, 256 (26 July, 1975), 109, 111.
—— *Philosophy*, 50 (1975), 373-4 ('Booknotes').
G. Ardley *Philosophical Studies* (Dublin), 27 (1980), 415-17.
J.L. Auspitz *Commentary*, 61: v (May 1976), 89-92, 94.
B.R. Barber *Government and Opposition*, 10 (1976), 446-63 ('Conserving politics: Michael Oakeshott and political theory').
J.A. Bradley *Heythrop Journal*, 18 (1977), 202-4.
B. Crick *Observer*, (20 April, 1975), 30.
H. Davis *New Behaviour*, (22 May, 1975), 231.
G.R. Dunstan *Law Quarterly Review*, 92 (1976), 122-6.
T. Fuller *Leviathan*, (17 October, 1976), 6-8.
—— *Journal of Politics*, 38 (1976), 184-6.
G. Gale *Spectator*, 234 (1975), 540.
G. Graham *Philosophical Quarterly*, 26 (1976), 201-3.
W. Hennis *Frankfurter Allgemeine Zeitung*, (18 March, 1976).
R.L. Hunt *Annals of the American Academy of Social and Political Science*, 430 (1977), 181-2.
D.A. Lloyd Thomas *Mind*, 86 (1977), 453-6.
D. Lopp *Philosophical Review*, 86 (1977), 235-8.
D.G. Macrae *Sunday Times*, (6 April, 1975), 38.
S. Miller *Partisan Review*, 44 (1977), 304-9.
K.R. Minogue *Quadrant*, 19: vii (October 1975), 77-83 ('Oakeshott and the idea of freedom').
F. Mount *National Review*, 27 (1975), 1301-2, 1304-5 ('Oakeshott's distinction').
G. Parry *Bibliographie de la Philosophie*, 23 (1976), 143.

Z. Pelczynski *Times Higher Education Supplement*, (23 May, 1975), 25.
D.D. Raphael *Political Quarterly*, 46 (1975), 450, 452, 454.
R. Rorty *Social Theory and Practice*, 4 (1976-8), 107-15.
L. Rubinoff *Canadian Journal of Political and Social Theory*, 3: ii (1979), 5-30 ('On theorizing human conduct').
A. Ryan *Listener*, 93 (1975), 517-18.
A. Seller *Philosophical Books*, 17 (1976), 54-7.
J. Shklar *Times Literary Supplement*, (12 September, 1975), 1018.
W. Vossenkuhl *Neue Bücher Zeitung*, (27 December, 1976), 12.
—— *Zeitschrift für Philosophische Forschung*, 31 (1977), 138-46 ('Die Lebensform des Menschen').
G.J. Warnock *Encounter*, 46 (April 1976), 84-7 ('The minefields of moral philosophy').
M. Warnock *New Society*, 32 (1 May, 1975), 288.

Reviews of 'On History and Other Essays' (1983)

Anon *Choice*, (July-August 1983), 1642.
—— *Critical Philosophy*, 12 (1983), 116.
—— *Osgoode Hall Law Journal*, 22 (Winter 1934), 794.
J.L. Auspitz *National Review*, 36 (10 February, 1984), 42, 44-8.
D.W. Bebbington *British Book News*, (August 1983), 522.
R.N. Berard *History Teacher* (Long Beach, California), 18 (1985), 449-51.
—— *International History Review*, 6 (1984), 301-3.
D. Boucher *History of Political Thought*, 5 (1984), 163-7.
J. Bradley *Heythrop Journal*, 27 (1986), 360-3.
E. Christiansen *Spectator*, 250 (9 April, 1983), 22-3.
W.H. Dray *Ethics*, 96 (1985-6), 197-8.
J. Dunn *History*, 70 (1985), 64.
R. Eccleshall *Political Studies*, 32 (1984), 167.
A. Esler *Social Science Journal*, 22 (1985), 135-6.
D.M. Fahey *Clio*, 14 (1984), 89-91.
R.A.D. Grant *Salisbury Review*, 3 (October 1984), 46-8.
J. Gray *Political Theory*, 12 (1984), 449-53.
G. Leff *English Historical Review*, 100 (1985), 953-4.
K.R. Minogue *American Spectator*, 16 (September 1983), 36-8.
P. Munz *European History Quarterly*, 14 (1984), 489-92.
H. Palmer *Philosophical Books*, 26 (1985), 117-20.
J.G.A. Pocock *Times Literary Supplement*, (21 October, 1983), 1155.
J. Sanderson *Durham University Journal*, 45 (1983-4), 315-17.
S.B. Smith *Review of Politics*, 47 (1985), 150-4.
W.A. Speck *Modern Language Review*, 79 (1984), 384-5.
B. Verschaffel *Tijdschrift voor Filosofie*, 47 (1985), 534-5.
W.H. Walsh *Times Higher Education Supplement*, (15 April, 1983), 16.

D. Weigall *Ideas and Production*, (1984), 93-5.

Reviews of 'The Voice of Liberal Learning: Michael Oakeshott on Education' (1989)

Anon *Economist*, 311 (22-28 April, 1989), 120, 125.
—— *Kenton, OH Times*, (16 February, 1989).
—— *Methodist Recorder*, (7 September, 1989).
—— *Publishers Weekly*, 235 (13 January, 1989), 81.
C. Bailey *Cambridge Journal of Education*, 20 (1990), 83-4.
D. Bromwich *New Republic*, 201 (3 July, 1989), 33-6.
R.F. Dearden *Journal of Educational Administration and History*, 2 (1990).
A. Flew *British Journal of Educational Studies*, 38 (1990), 386-8.
I. Gilmour *London Review of Books*, 12 (12 July, 1990), 8-9.
W.H. Greenleaf *Times Higher Education Supplement*, (6 July, 1990), 18.
T. Hall *Review of Metaphysics*, 43 (1989-90), 159-61.
W.E. Hall *Birmingham Post*, (25 May, 1989).
P. Johnson *Utilitas*, 4 (1992), 178-81.
B.A. Kimball *American Journal of Education*, 98 (1990), 251-69 ('Professions of language and reason').
C. Moore *Spectator*, 262 (17 June, 1989), 27-8.
F. Mount *Sunday Telegraph*, (23 April, 1989).
D.G. Myers *American Scholar*, 59 (1989-90), 626-8.
A. O'Hear *Salisbury Review*, 8 (September 1989), 64-5.
J. Passmore *Times Literary Supplement*, (26 May, 1989), 567-8.
J.E. Powell *Independent*, (9 March, 1989), 28.
J.R. Searle *New York Review of Books*, 37 (6 December, 1990), 34-42.
R.R. Sherman *Change*, 21 (July 1989), 61.
—— *Choice*, 26 (July 1989), 1882.
J. Sobran *National Review*, 42 (16 April, 1990), 50-1.
A. Sullivan *Wall Street Journal*, (31 May, 1989).
S. Walsh *Oxford Times*, (17 March, 1989).
K. Williams *Studies in Education: a Journal of Educational Research*, 7 (Autumn 1990), 68-70.

Reviews of 'Rationalism in Politics and other Essays' (1991)

Anon *First Things*, (March 1992), 53.
—— *Wisconsin Bookwatch*, 1:ix (September 1991), 1-2.
R.A. Peterson *Freeman*, (June 1992), 246-7.
J.E. Powell *Economic Affairs*, (November 1991).

Bibliography

B. Other Published Work

F.J. Abbate *A Preface to the Philosophy of the State* (Belmont, California: Wadsworth Publishing Co., 1977).

J. Abse (ed.) *My LSE* (London: Robson Books, 1977).

H.B. Acton 'Tradition and some other forms of order', *Proceedings of the Aristotelian Society*, n.s. 53 (1952-3), 1-28.

N. Annan 'Revulsion to the right', *Political Quarterly*, 26 (1955), 211-19.

—— *Our Age: Portrait of a Generation* (London: Weidenfeld and Nicolson, 1990).

Anon 'New directions', *Observer*, (8 October, 1950).

—— 'He succeeds Laski', *Daily Express*, (13 October, 1950).

—— 'Right turn', *Evening Standard*, (13 October, 1950).

—— 'Chair of Political Science', *Manchester Guardian*, (17 October, 1950).

—— 'Knowledge v. pet ideas', *Time*, 56 (23 October, 1950), 60-2.

—— 'Reducing risk of false ideas', *Manchester Guardian*, (7 March, 1951).

—— 'Bathing in the nude ...', *Sunday Pictorial*, (9 October, 1955).

—— 'Profile: Professor Oakeshott', *Clare Market Review*, 54: i (Michaelmas 1958 and Lent 1959), 14.

—— Review of *Politics and Experience*, ed. P. King and B.C. Parekh, in *Times Literary Supplement*, (13 February, 1969), 150.

—— 'Michael Oakeshott', *LSE*, 37 (June 1969), 16.

—— 'Philosopher of conversation', *Spectator*, 254 (25 May, 1985), 18-19.

—— Obituary, *Daily Telegraph*, (21 December, 1990), 19.

—— 'Academics remember Oakeshott', *Times*, (22 December, 1990), 3.

—— 'Pragmatic Thatcherite' (leader), *Times*, (22 December, 1990), 9.

—— Obituary, *Times*, (22 December, 1990), 10.

—— Obituary, *L.A. Times*, (December 1990).

—— 'Memorial service', *Times*, (21 October, 1991), 16.

J.R. Archer 'Oakeshott on politics', *Journal of Politics*, 41 (1979), 150-68.

N. Ashford 'Michael Oakeshott and the Conservative Disposition', *Intercollegiate Review*, 25 (Spring 1990), 39-50.

M. Asthana 'Michael Oakeshott against scientism in politics', *Modern Review* (Calcutta), 131 (1972), 409-14.

R.F. Atkinson *Knowledge and Explanation in History: an Introduction to the Philosophy of History* (London: Macmillan, 1978).

Atticus 'Gale force six', *Sunday Times*, (1 November, 1970).

J.L. Auspitz 'Individuality, civility and theory: the philosophical imagination of Michael Oakeshott', *Political Theory*, 4 (1976), 261-94.

—— 'Michael Oakeshott: 1901-1990', *American Scholar*, 60 (1990-1), 351-70. Chapter 1 above.

P. Bahners 'Auf hoher See. Zum Tode des Philosophen Michael Oakeshott', *Frankfurter Allgemeine Zeitung*, (28 December, 1990), 1 and 25.
B. Barber *The Conquest of Politics. Liberal Philosophy in Democratic Times* (Princeton: Princeton University Press, 1988).
R. Barker *Political Ideas in Modern Britain* (London: Methuen, 1978).
G. Barraclough Review of *Politics and Experience*, ed. P. King and B.C. Parekh, in *Spectator*, 222 (1969), 144-6; correspondence, 253.
B. Barry *Political Argument* (London: Routledge and Kegan Paul, 1965).
W. Baumgarth 'Habit and discovery: the political philosophy of Michael Oakeshott', *Political Science Reviewer*, 7 (1977), 273-323.
M. Beloff Review of *Politics and Experience*, ed. P. King and B.C. Parekh, in *Cambridge Review*, 90 (1969), 239-40.
—— 'Universities and the public purse: an update' *Higher Education Quarterly*, 44 (1990-1), 3-20.
S.I. Benn & R.S Peters *Social Principles and the Democratic State* (London: George Allen and Unwin, 1959).
R. Bennett 'The Professor likes Good Brandy', *Evening Standard*, (4 June, 1959).
R.N. Berki *The History of Political Thought: a Short Introduction* (London: Dent, 1977).
—— *On Political Realism* (London: Dent, 1981).
—— 'Oakeshott's conception of civil association: notes for a critical analysis', *Political Studies*, 29 (1981), 570-85.
A.H. Birch 'Historical explanation and the study of politics', *Government and Opposition*, 4 (1969), 215-30.
C. Blake 'Can history be objective?', in *Theories of History*, ed. P.L. Gardiner (Glencoe, Illinois: The Free Press, 1959), pp. 329-43.
L. Bloch Correspondence, *Daily Telegraph*, (4 March, 1977).
—— Correspondence, *Daily Telegraph*, (10 July, 1978).
J.G. Blumler 'Politics, poetry and practice', *Political Studies*, 12 (1964), 356-61.
D. Boucher Review of *The History of Ideas*, ed. P. King, in *History of Political Thought*, 5 (1984), 154-8.
—— 'The creation of the past: British idealism and Michael Oakeshott's philosophy of history', *History and Theory*, 23 (1984), 193-214.
—— *Texts in Context: Revisionist Methods for Studying the History of Ideas* (Dordrecht: Martinus Nijhoff Publishers, 1985).
—— 'W.H. Greenleaf, idealism and the triadic conception of the history of political thought', *Idealistic Studies*, 16 (1986), 237-52.
—— 'Overlap and autonomy: the different worlds of Collingwood and Oakeshott', *Storia*, 4 (1989), 69-89.
—— 'Politics in a different mode: an appreciation of Michael Oakeshott', *History of Political Thought*, 12 (1991), 717-28.
J. Bowle *Minos or Minotaur?* (London: Cape, 1956).

C. Brooke Obituary, *Independent*, (29 December 1990).
—— Obituary, *Caian*, (November 1991), 103-4.
J.M. Brown 'A note on Professor Oakeshott's Introduction to the *Leviathan*', *Political Studies*, 1 (1953), 53-64.
—— 'Hobbes: a rejoinder', *Political Studies*, 2 (1954), 168-72.
J. Burns 'Viewpoint', *Cambridge Review*, 112 (October 1991), 133-6.
W. Buckley *American Conservative Thought in the Twentieth Century* (New York: Bobbs Merrill, 1970).
J.M.C. 'Professor Michael Oakeshott: a personal impression', *Clare Market Review*, 46: ii (Lent 1951), 39-40.
D. Campbell 'The FO and the eggheads', *New Statesman*, 101 (27 February, 1981), 13-14.
E.H. Carr *What is History?* (London: Macmillan, 1962).
J. Casey *Pagan Virtue: an Essay in Ethics* (Clarendon Press: Oxford, 1990).
—— Obituary, *Daily Telegraph*, (21 December, 1990), 19.
—— 'Mankind in conversation: the philosophy of Michael Oakeshott and its misunderstandings', *Times Literary Supplement*, (29 March, 1991), 3-4 (review of R. Grant, *Oakeshott*).
—— Obituary, *Caian*, (November 1991), 97-103. Chapter 4 above.
G.E.G. Catlin Correspondence, *Modern Churchman*, 19 (1929-30), 614.
—— 'Contemporary British political thought', *American Political Science Review*, 46 (1952), 641-59.
J. Charvet *A Critique of Freedom and Equality* (Cambridge: Cambridge University Press, 1981).
W.J. Coats, Jr. 'Michael Oakeshott as liberal theorist', *Canadian Journal of Political Science*, 18 (1985), 773-87. Reprinted in W.J. Coats, Jr. *The Activity of Politics and Related Essays* (Selinsgrove: Susquehanna University Press, 1989), pp. 42-57.
—— 'Michael Oakeshott's critique of Rationalism in politics', in *The Activity of Politics and Related Essays, op. cit.*
—— 'Some correspondence between Oakeshott's "Civil Condition" and the Republican Tradition', *Political Science Reviewer*, 21 (1992), (forthcoming).
A. Cobban 'History and sociology', *Historical Studies*, 3 (1961), 1-8.
S. Coleman 'Is there reason in tradition?', in *Politics and Experience*, ed. P. King and B.C. Parekh (Cambridge: Cambridge University Press, 1968), pp. 239-82.
R.G. Collingwood *The Idea of History* (Oxford: Oxford University Press, 1946).
C. Covell 'Practices and persons: Strawson and Oakeshott', *Cambridge Review*, 100 (1978), 167-72.
—— *The Redefinition of Conservatism: Politics and Doctrine* (Basingstoke: Macmillan, 1986).
M. Cowling *The Nature and Limits of Political Science* (Cambridge: Cambridge University Press, 1963).

—— *Religion and Public Doctrine in Modern England* (Cambridge: Cambridge University Press, 1980).
—— 'The sources of the New Right: irony, geniality and malice', *Encounter*, (November 1989), 3-13.
M. Cranston 'Michael Oakeshott: a conservative sceptic', *Encounter*, 28 (January 1967), 82-6.
—— 'Remembrances of Michael Oakeshott', *Political Theory*, 19 (1991), 323-6.
J.M. Creed *The Divinity of Jesus Christ* (Cambridge: Cambridge University Press, 1938).
B. Crick 'The world of Michael Oakeshott: or the lonely nihilist', *Encounter*, 20 (June 1963), 65-6, 68, 70-4.
—— *In Defence of Politics* (Harmondsworth, Middlesex: Penguin, 1964).
—— Review of W.H. Greenleaf, *Oakeshott's Philosophical Politics*, in *New Society*, 8 (1966), 622.
—— Correspondence, *Times Literary Supplement*, (13 January, 1978), 37.
—— 'Ideal scourge of the idealists' (obituary), *Guardian*, (22 December, 1990), 19.
—— 'The ambiguity of Michael Oakeshott', *Cambridge Review*, 112 (October 1991), 120-4.
D. Davie 'Politics and literature: John Adams and Doctor Johnson', in *Politics and Experience*, ed. P. King and B.C. Parekh (Cambridge: Cambridge University Press, 1968), pp. 395-408.
H. Davis 'Poetry and the voice of Michael Oakeshott', *British Journal of Aesthetics*, 15 (1975), 59-68.
A. Donagan *The Later Philosophy of R.G. Collingwood* (Oxford: Oxford University Press, 1962).
J. Doughty 'The Spectator's View', *Daily Telegraph*, (28 December, 1990).
R.E. Dowling 'Oakeshott's theory of reason, tradition and conservatism', *Australian Journal of Politics and History*, 5 (1959), 51-63.
W.H. Dray *Laws and Explanations in History* (Oxford: Oxford University Press, 1957).
—— *Philosophy of History* (Englewood Cliffs, N.J.: Prentice-Hall, 1964).
—— 'Michael Oakeshott's theory of history', in *Politics and Experience*, ed. P. King and B.C. Parekh (Cambridge: Cambridge University Press, 1968), pp. 19-42.
—— 'On the nature and role of narrative in history', *History and Theory*, 10 (1971), 153-71.
H.M. Drucker *The Political Uses of Ideology* (London: Macmillan, 1974).
F. Dunlop 'Human nature, learning and ideology', *British Journal of Educational Studies*, 25 (1977), 239-57.
K. Dyson *The State Tradition in Western Europe* (Oxford: Martin

Bibliography

Robertson, 1980).
G.R. Elton *Political History* (London: Allen Lane, 1970).
H.C. Ewing Obituary, *Independent*, (29 December, 1990).
G. Feaver 'Michael Oakeshott and political education', *Studies in Comparative Communism*, 2 (1969), 156-75.
—— 'The enduring and elusive legacy of Michael Oakeshott', *Studies in Political Thought*, 1 (1992), 95-121.
R.E. Flathman *The Practice of Political Authority: Authority and the Authoritative* (Chicago: University of Chicago Press, 1980).
—— *Toward a Liberalism* ... (London: Cornell University Press, 1989).
A. Flew Review of W.H. Greenleaf, *Oakeshott's Philosophical Politics*, in *Spectator*, 218 (1967), 108-9.
G. Fowler Obituary, *New York Times*, (22 December, 1990), 33.
P. Franco *The Political Philosophy of Michael Oakeshott* (New Haven and London: Yale University Press, 1990).
—— Correspondence, *Times Literary Supplement*, (10-16 August, 1990), 847.
—— 'Michael Oakeshott as a liberal theorist', *Political Theory*, 18 (1990), 411-36.
—— 'Oakeshott's critique of Rationalism revisited', *Political Science Reviewer*, 21 (1992), (forthcoming).
R.B. Friedman 'Oakeshott on the authority of law', *Ratio Juris*, 2 (1989), 27-40.
—— 'What is a non-instrumental law?', *Political Science Reviewer*, 21 (1992), (forthcoming).
T. Fuller 'Conversational gambits in political theory: Yves Simon's great dialogue', *Political Theory*, 10 (1982), 566-79.
—— 'Authority and the individual in civil association: Oakeshott, Flathman and Yves Simon', in *Authority Revisited* (Nomos 29), ed. J.R. Pennock and J.W. Chapman (New York and London: New York University Press, 1987).
—— Introduction to *The Voice of Liberal Learning: Michael Oakeshott on Education*, ed. T. Fuller (New Haven and London: Yale University Press, 1989), pp. 1-16.
—— 'Response to Kimball', *American Journal of Education*, 98 (1990), 274-7.
—— Correspondence, *Times Literary Supplement*, (27 July – 2 August, 1990), 799.
—— Foreword and Bibliography to *Rationalism in Politics and Other Essays* (new and expanded edition), ed. T. Fuller (Indianapolis: Liberty Press, 1991), pp. xii – xxvi.
—— 'The Work of Michael Oakeshott', *Political Theory*, 19 (1991), 326-33. Chapter 5 above.
—— 'The Work of Michael Oakeshott', *The Disparaging Eye* (Colorado College), (October/November 1991), 23-6.
—— 'An introduction: Michael Oakeshott's achievement', *Political Science Reviewer*, 21 (1992), (forthcoming).

W.A. Galston *Justice and the Human Good* (Chicago and London: University of Chicago Press, 1980).

A. Gamble *The Conservative Nation* (London: Routledge and Kegan Paul, 1974).

P.L. Gardiner *The Nature of Historical Explanation* (Oxford: Oxford University Press, 1961).

P. de Gaudemar 'Note sur Thomas Hobbes', *Revue Internationale sur Philosophie*, 4 (1949), 452-9.

D.P. Gauthier *The Logic of Leviathan: the Moral and Political Theory of Thomas Hobbes* (Oxford: Clarendon Press, 1969).

E. Gellner *Thought and Change* (London: Weidenfeld and Nicolson, 1964).

—— *Contemporary Thought and Politics* (London: Routledge and Kegan Paul, 1974).

—— *Legitimation of Belief* (Cambridge: Cambridge University Press, 1974).

—— *Spectacles and Predicaments. Essays in Social Theory* (Cambridge: Cambridge University Press, 1979).

—— 'The LSE – a contested academy', *Times Higher Education Supplement*, no. 418 (7 November, 1980), 12-13.

—— *Relativism and the Social Sciences* (Cambridge: Cambridge University Press, 1985).

D. Germino *Beyond Ideology. The Revival of Political Theory* (New York: Harper and Row, 1967).

A. Giddens *The Constitution of Society* (Cambridge: Polity Press, 1984).

H. Gilliam 'The dialectics of realism and idealism in modern historiographic theory', *History and Theory*, 15 (1976), 231-56.

I. Gilmour *Inside Right. A Study of Conservatism* (London: Hutchinson, 1977).

D.S. Goldstein 'J.B. Bury's philosophy of history: a reappraisal' *American Historical Review*, 82 (1977), 896-919.

G. Graham 'Practical politics and philosophical inquiry', *Philosophical Quarterly*, 28 (1978), 234-41.

—— 'Reply to Liddington', *Philosophical Quarterly*, 28 (1978), 157.

—— *Politics in its Place: a Study of Six Ideologies* (Oxford: Oxford University Press, 1986).

R.A.D. Grant 'Conservative thinkers: Michael Oakeshott: the poet of practice', *Salisbury Review*, 1 (Spring 1983), 12-16.

—— 'Oakeshott', in *Conservative Thinkers*, ed. R. Scruton (London: The Claridge Press, 1988), pp. 275-94.

—— *Oakeshott* (London: The Claridge Press, 1990).

—— 'Inside the hedge: Oakeshott's early life and work', *Cambridge Review*, 112 (October 1991), 106-9.

J.N. Gray 'F.A. Hayek on liberty and tradition', *Journal of Libertarian Studies*, 4 (1980), 119-37.

—— 'Hayek on liberty, rights, and justice', *Ethics*, 92 (1981), 73-84.

—— *Hayek on Liberty* (Oxford: Basil Blackwell, 1984).

—— 'Oakeshott on law, liberty and civil association', *The World and I*, (September 1988) reprinted in *Liberalisms: Essays in Political Philosophy* (London: Routledge, 1989), pp. 199-216.

—— 'Michael Oakeshott and the political economy of freedom', *The World and I*, (September 1988).

—— *Limited Government: a Positive Agenda* (London: Institute of Economic Affairs, 1989).

—— 'Oakeshott as a liberal', *Salisbury Review*, 10 (September 1991), 22-5.

H.R.G. Greaves *The Foundations of Political Theory* (London: London School of Economics and Political Science, 1966; 2nd ed.).

W.H. Greenleaf *Oakeshott's Philosophical Politics* (London: Longmans, 1966.

—— 'Idealism, modern philosophy and politics' in *Politics and Experience*, ed. P. King and B.C. Parekh (Cambridge: Cambridge University Press, 1968), pp. 93-124.

—— Review of R. Singh, *Reason, Revolution and Political Theory*, in *Political Studies*, 16 (1968), 456-7.

—— 'Algunas relaciones entre la idea de decadencia y pensamiento conservador en la Europa moderna', *Alternativas* (Santiago, Chile), (June 1984), 7-71.

—— Review of P. Franco, *The Political Philosophy of Michael Oakeshott*, in *Times Higher Education Supplement*, (6 July, 1990), 18.

D. Hall & T. Modood 'Practical politics and philosophical inquiry: a note', *Philosophical Quarterly*, 29 (1979), 340-4.

—— 'Oakeshott and the impossibility of philosophical politics', *Political Studies*, 30 (1982), 157-76.

—— 'A reply to Liddington', *Political Studies*, 30 (1982), 184-9.

T. H[all] 'Michael Oakeshott, R.I.P.', *Crisis* (March 1991).

J. Hamburger Review of W.H. Greenleaf, *Oakeshott's Philosophical Politics*, in *American Political Science Review*, 61 (1967), 782-3.

C.M. Hamm 'Can moral judgment be taught?', *Journal of Educational Thought*, 8 (1974), 73-86.

M. Harrington 'The real LSE behind the myths', *Daily Telegraph*, (6 December, 1972).

J. Hart 'Two paths home: Kendall and Oakeshott', *Triumph*, 2: x (October 1967), 28-30, 32-4.

—— 'Michael Oakeshott, RIP', *National Review*, 43 (28 January, 1991), 19-20. Chapter 6 above.

W.C. Havard 'Michael Oakeshott', in *Der Gebändigte Kapitalismus: Sozialisten und Konservative im Wohlfahrtstaat. Englisches Politisches Denken im 20 Jahrhundert* (Munich, 1974), pp. 71-98.

—— *The Recovery of Political Theory: Limits and Possibilities* (Baton Rouge and London: Louisiana State University Press, 1984).

F.A. Hayek *Law, Legislation and Liberty* (London: Routledge and Kegan Paul, 1973, 1976, 1979).

T. Hegert 'CC Prof persuaded colleague to share well-educated ideas', *Gazette Telegraph* (Colorado Springs), (7 March, 1989).

G.P. Henderson 'A survey of work dealing with 17th and 18th century British Empiricism, 1945-1950', *Philosophical Quarterly*, 1 (1951), 254-68.

R.J. Hills *Phantom was There*.

G. Himmelfarb 'The Conservative imagination: Michael Oakeshott', *American Scholar*, 44 (1974-5), 405-20. Reprinted as 'Michael Oakeshott: the conservative disposition' in G. Himmelfarb, *Marriage and Morals among the Victorians* (New York: Alfred Knopf, 1986), pp. 210-30.

—— ' "Supposing history is a woman – what then?" ', *American Scholar*, 53 (1983-4), 494-505. Reprinted as 'Does history talk sense?' in G. Himmelfarb, *The New History and the Old* (Cambridge, Massachusetts: Harvard University Press, 1987), pp. 171-84.

I. Holliday 'On Michael Oakeshott', *Government and Opposition*, 27 (1992), 131-47.

T. Honderich *Conservatism* (London: Hamish Hamilton, 1990).

P. Howard 'Donnish fury blazes at politics of judiciary', *Times*, (31 January, 1978), 1.

N. Johnson 'Die politische philosophie Michael Oakeshotts', *Zeitschrift für Politik*, 32 (1985), 347-74.

P. Johnson Review of P. Franco, *The Political Philosophy of Michael Oakeshott*, in *Utilitas*, 4 (1992), 178-81.

W.M. Johnston *The Formative Years of R.G. Collingwood* (The Hague: Martinus Nijhoff, 1967).

H.S. Kariel *In Search of Authority: Twentieth Century Political Thought* (Glencoe: The Free Press, 1964).

H.D. Kellner 'Time out: the discontinuity of historical consciousness', *History and Theory*, 14 (1975), 275-96.

J. Kemp Review of *Philosophy, Politics and Society*, ed. P. Laslett, in *Philosophical Quarterly*, 7 (1957), 276-83.

M.D. King 'Reason, tradition and the progressiveness of science', *History and Theory*, 10 (1971), 3-32.

P. King 'Michael Oakeshott and historical particularism', *Politics*, 16 (1981), 85-102. Reprinted in *The History of Ideas*, ed. P. King (London: Croom Helm, 1983).

P. King & B.C. Parekh (eds.) *Politics and Experience. Essays Presented to Professor Michael Oakeshott on the Occasion of his Retirement* (Cambridge: Cambridge University Press, 1968).

G.E. Kneller *Movements of Thought in Modern Education* (New York: John Wiley and Sons, 1984).

R.A. Kocis 'Reason, development and the conflicts of human ends: Sir Isaiah Berlin's vision of politics', *American Political Science Review*, 74 (1980), 38-52.

K.E. Koerner *Liberalism and its Critics* (London: Croom Helm, 1985).
D. Krook 'Rationalism in politics: a comment', *Cambridge Journal*, 1 (1947-8), 439-47.
—— 'Mr. Brown's Note annotated', *Political Studies*, 1 (1953), 216- 27.
—— 'Rationalism triumphant: an essay on the kibbutzim of Israel', in *Politics and Experience*, ed. P. King and B.C. Parekh (Cambridge: Cambridge University Press, 1968), pp. 309-40.
C. Kukathas *Hayek and Modern Liberalism* (Oxford: Clarendon Press, 1989).
H. Kuhn 'Der Staat, philosophisch betrachtet', *Philosophische Rundschau*, 28 (1981), 221-8.
E.F. de Ledesma Correspondence, *Daily Telegraph*, (10 July, 1978).
S.R. Letwin 'Rationalism, principles and politics', *Review of Politics*, 14 (1952), 367-93.
—— 'Morality and law', *Encounter*, 43 (November 1974), 35-43. Reprinted in *Ratio Juris*, 2 (1989), 55-65.
—— Correspondence, *Daily Telegraph*, (28 January, 1977).
—— 'On conservative individualism', in *Conservative Essays*, ed. M. Cowling (London: Cassell, 1978), pp. 52-68.
—— *The Gentleman in Trollope: Individuality and Moral Conduct* (London: Macmillan, 1982).
—— Correspondence, *Times Literary Supplement*, (2-9 March, 1990), 223.
W. von Leyden 'Categories of historical understanding', *History and Theory*, 23 (1984), 53-77.
J. Liddington 'Graham on politics and philosophy', *Philosophical Quarterly*, 29 (1979), 153-6.
—— 'Hall and Modood on Oakeshott', *Political Studies*, 30 (1982), 177-86.
—— 'Oakeshott: freedom in the modern European state', in *Concepts of Liberty in Political Theory*, ed. J.N. Gray and Z. Pelczynski (London: Athlone Press, 1984), pp. 289-320.
M. Lilla 'On Goodman, Putnam and Rorty: the return to the "given" ', *Partisan Review*, 51 (1984), 220-35.
A. Lockyer 'Traditions as context in the history of political theory', *Political Studies*, 27 (1979), 201-17.
A. Lugg 'Was Wittgenstein a conservative thinker?' *Southern Journal of Philosophy*, 23 (1985), 465-74.
D.N. MacCormick 'Spontaneous order and the rule of law: some problems', *Ratio Juris*, 2 (1989), 41-54.
C.B. McCullagh 'Narration and explanation in history', *Mind*, 78 (1969), 256-61.
S. Macedo *Liberal Virtues: Citizenship, Virtue and Community in Liberal Constitutionalism* (Oxford: Clarendon Press, 1990).
J. Mack 'The LSE: a monument to Fabian socialism?', *New Society*, 44 (15 June, 1978), 588-91.

W.J.M. Mackenzie *Politics and Social Science* (Harmondsworth, Middlesex: Penguin, 1967).

G. McLennan 'History and theory: contemporary debates and directions', *Literature and History*, 10 (1984), 139-64.

F.S. McNeilly Review of W.H. Greenleaf, *Oakeshott's Philosophical Politics*, in *Philosophical Books*, 8 (1967), 4-6.

C.B. Macpherson Review of *Politics and Experience*, ed. P. King and B.C. Parekh, in *Political Science Quarterly*, 36 (1971), 310-11.

T. McPherson Review of W.H. Greenleaf, *Oakeshott's Philosophical Politics*, in *Political Studies*, 15 (1967), 373.

M. Mandelbaum *The Anatomy of Historical Knowledge* (London: Johns Hopkins University Press, 1977).

D.J. Manning 'Professor Michael Oakeshott's contribution to political thought', *Clare Market* (elsewhere *Clare Market Review*), (Lent 1965), 27-34.

—— 'Michael Oakeshott's contribution to political thought', *Kolokon* (Durham), 1 (Spring 1966), 36-42 (abridged version of above).

—— *The Mind of Jeremy Bentham* (London: Longmans, 1968).

—— 'The place of ideology in political life', in *The Form of Ideology*, ed. D.J. Manning (London: George Allen and Unwin, 1980), pp. 71-89.

D.J. Manning & T.J. Robinson *The Place of Ideology in Political Life* (London: Croom Helm, 1985).

D.R. Mapel 'Civil association and the idea of contingency', *Political Theory*, 18 (1990), 392-410.

—— 'Purpose and politics: can there be a non-instrumental civil association?', *Political Science Reviewer*, 21 (1992), (forthcoming).

A. Marwick *The Nature of History* (London: Macmillan, 1970).

A. Maude *The Common Problem* (London: Constable, 1969).

J.L. Mayer 'Managers, Machiavelli, and Oakeshott, M. – caveat', *Publius, the Journal of Federalism*, 6: iv (1976), 101-5.

J.W. Meiland *Scepticism and Historical Knowledge* (New York: Random House, 1965).

H. Mewes 'Individualism in Oakeshott, Arendt and Strauss', *Political Science Reviewer*, 21 (1992), (forthcoming).

K.R. Minogue *The Liberal Mind* (London: Methuen, 1963).

—— 'Conservatism', in *The Encyclopedia of Philosophy*, ed. P. Edwards (London: Collier-Macmillan, 1967), ii, 195-8.

—— 'Revolution, tradition and political continuity', in *Politics and Experience*, ed. P. King and B.C. Parekh (Cambridge: Cambridge University Press, 1968), pp. 283-308.

—— *The Concept of a University* (London: Weidenfeld and Nicolson, 1973).

—— 'Parts and wholes: twentieth century interpretation of Thomas Hobbes', *Annales de la Catedra Francisco Suarez*, número 14, fascículo único 1974, 77-108.

—— 'Michael Oakeshott: the boundless sea of politics', in *Contem-*

porary Political Philosophers, ed. A. de Crespigny and K.R. Minogue (London: Methuen, 1976), pp. 120-46.

—— 'Michael Oakeshott (1901-1990)', *LSE Magazine*, 3 (Summer 1991) 16-17.

—— 'A memoir: Michael Oakeshott (1901-1990)', *Political Studies*, 39 (1991), 369-77. Chapter 3 above.

—— 'Michael Oakeshott and the history of political thought seminar', *Cambridge Review*, 112 (October 1991), 114-17. Chapter 7 above.

W. Moberly 'The universities', *Cambridge Journal*, 3 (1949-50), 195-213.

T. Modood 'Oakeshott's conceptions of philosophy', *Indian Journal of Political Science*, 40 (1979), 478-86.

—— 'Oakeshott's conceptions of philosophy', *History of Political Thought*, 1 (1980), 315-22 (revised version of above).

C. Moore 'The sea-captain who threw his coat into the stormy sea and said, "Take that!"', *Spectator*, 266 (15 June, 1991), 8.

A. Moulakis 'Consciousness and history', *Rivista Internazionale di Filosofia del Diritto*, 66 (1989), 450-67.

D.H. Munro 'Godwin, Oakeshott, and Mrs. Bloomer', *Journal of History of Ideas*, 35 (1974), 611-24.

I. Murdoch 'A house of theory', *Partisan Review*, 26 (1959), 17-31.

T. Nagel 'Hobbes's concept of obligation', *Philosophical Review*, 68 (1959), 68-83.

R.F. Nagel Review of L.H. Tribe, *American Constitutional Law*, in *University of Pennsylvania Law Review*, 127 (1979), 1174-94.

J. Nardin 'The social critic in Trollope's novels', *Studies in English Literature, 1500-1900*, 30 (1990), 679-96.

T. Nardin 'Distributive justice and the criticism of international law', *Political Studies*, 29 (1981), 232-44.

—— *Law, Morality and the Relations of States* (Princeton: Princeton University Press, 1983).

D.L. Norton 'Tradition and autonomous individuality', *Journal of Value Enquiry*, 21 (1987), 131-40.

—— *Democracy and Moral Development* (Oxford: University of California Press, 1991).

P. Norton & A. Aughey *Conservatives and Conservatism* (London: Temple Smith, 1981).

J.C. Nyiri 'Wittgenstein's later work in relation to conservatism', in *Wittgenstein and His Times*, ed. B. McGuinness (Oxford: Basil Blackwell, 1982), pp. 44-68.

A. Oldfield 'Michael Oakeshott', in *The Fontana Biographical Companion to Modern Thought*, ed. A. Bullock and R.B. Woodings (London: Fontana, 1983), p. 562.

L. Ornaghi 'Dall' "ambivalenza" dello stato moderno all'analisi della condotta umana. Michael Oakeshott e la ricerca politica contemporanea', *Annali dell'Istituto Storico Italo-Germanico in Trento*, 5 (1979), 279-307.

R. Orr Review of R. Grant, *Oakeshott*, in *LSE Magazine*, 32.
—— 'A double agent in the dream of Michael Oakeshott', *Political Science Reviewer*, 21 (1992), (forthcoming).
J.W. Osborne 'Anthony Powell and Michael Oakeshott', *Modern Age*, 29 (1985), 380-2.
N.K. O'Sullivan *Conservatism* (London: Dent, 1976).
—— *The Problem of Political Obligation* (New York and London: Garland Press, 1987).
—— Obituary, *Independent*, (22 December, 1990). Chapter 9 above.
B. Page 'London Diary', *New Statesman*, (8 February, 1980).
B. Page, D. Leitch & P. Knightley *Philby: The Spy who Betrayed a Generation* (London: Sphere Books, 1977).
B.C. Parekh, see also P. King
—— 'The nature of political philosophy', in *Politics and Experience*, ed. P. King and B.C. Parekh (Cambridge: Cambridge University Press, 1968), pp. 153-208.
—— 'The political philosophy of Michael Oakeshott', *British Journal of Political Science*, 9 (1979), 481-506.
—— *Contemporary Political Thinkers* (Oxford: Martin Robertson, 1982).
—— 'Oakeshott, Michael Joseph', in *The Blackwell Encyclopaedia of Political Thought*, ed. D. Miller (Oxford: Basil Blackwell, 1987), 359-60.
—— Review of P. Franco, *The Political Philosophy of Michael Oakeshott*, in *Political Studies*, 38 (1990), 723-4.
—— Obituary, *Independent*, (22 December, 1990).
—— 'Living as an immortal', *Cambridge Review*, 112 (October 1991), 99-106.
G. Parry 'Tradition, community and self-determination', *British Journal of Political Science*, 12 (1982), 399-419.
T.P. Peardon 'Two currents in contemporary English political theory', *American Political Science Review*, 49 (1955), 487-95.
J.R. Peden 'Michael Oakeshott', in *Cyclopedia of World Authors* (vol. 2), ed. F.N. Magill.
R.S. Peters, see also S.I. Benn
—— *Ethics and Education* (London: George Allen and Unwin, 1966).
—— 'Michael Oakeshott's philosophy of education', in *Politics and Experience*, ed. P. King and B.C. Parekh (Cambridge: Cambridge University Press, 1968), pp. 43-64.
—— *Authority, Responsibility and Education* (London: George Allen and Unwin, 1973; 3rd. ed.).
—— *Psychology and Ethical Development* (London: George Allen and Unwin, 1974).
W. Pickles Correspondence, *Encounter*, 21 (September 1963), 89.
N. Pilling 'The Conservatism of Sir Henry Maine', *Political Studies*, 18 (1970), 107-20.
H.F. Pitkin *Wittgenstein and Justice: the Significance of Ludwig*

Wittgenstein for Social and Political Thought (Berkeley: University of California Press, 1972).

—— 'The roots of conservatism: Michael Oakeshott and the denial of politics', *Dissent*, 20 (1973), 496-525. Reprinted in *The New Conservatism: a Critique from the Left*, ed. L.A. Coser and I. Howe (New York, 1974), pp. 243-88.

—— 'Inhuman conduct and unpolitical theory: Michael Oakeshott's *On Human Conduct*', *Political Theory*, 4 (1976), 301-20.

R. Plant *Hegel* (London: George Allen and Unwin, 1973).

J.G.A. Pocock 'Time, institutions and action: an essay on traditions and their understanding', in *Politics and Experience*, ed. P. King and B.C. Parekh (Cambridge: Cambridge University Press, 1968), pp. 209-38.

M. Postan 'The revulsion from thought', *Cambridge Journal*, 1 (1947-8), 395-408.

R. Price 'Memories of Michael Oakeshott', *Cambridge Review*, 112 (October 1991), 117-20. Chapter 2 above.

A. Quinton *The Politics of Imperfection* (London: Faber and Faber, 1978).

D.D. Raphael '*Rationalism in Politics*: a note on Professor Oakeshott's reply', *Political Studies*, 13 (1965), 395-7.

L.S. Rathore & P.S. Bhati 'Political ideas of Michael Oakeshott', *Indian Journal of Political Studies*, 3-4 (1980), 254-64.

J.D. Rayner 'The use of ideological language', in *The Form of Ideology*, ed. D.J. Manning (London: George Allen and Unwin, 1980), pp. 90-112.

—— 'The legend of Oakeshott's conservatism: sceptical philosophy and limited politics', *Canadian Journal of Political Science*, 18 (1985), 313-38.

H.S. Reiss 'Konservatives Denken in England. Zur Politischen von Michael Oakeshott', *Studium Generale* (Berlin), 10 (1957), 161-5.

G.J. Renier *History, its Purpose and Method* (London: George Allen and Unwin, 1950).

K. Reschauer Review of *Politics and Experience*, ed. P. King and B.C. Parekh, in *Canadian Journal of Political Science*, 3 (1970), 167-8.

P. Riley 'Michael Oakeshott', in *Conference for the Study of Political Thought International Newsletter*, 20: ii (1991), 1-2, 9-11.

—— 'Michael Oakeshott, political philosopher', *Cambridge Review*, 112 (October 1991), 110-13.

—— 'The voice of Michael Oakeshott in the conversation of mankind', *Political Theory*, 19 (1991), 334-5.

R. Rorty *Philosophy and the Mirror of Nature* (Princeton: Princeton University Press, 1979).

—— *Contingency, Irony, and Solidarity* (Cambridge: Cambridge University Press, 1989).

K. Rose 'Albany at large', *Sunday Telegraph*, (14 November, 1982), 2.

—— 'Albany at large', *Sunday Telegraph*, (10 February, 1985), 2.

N. Rotenstreich *Philosophy, History and Politics. Studies in Contemporary English Philosophy of History* (The Hague: Martinus Nijhoff, 1976).

L. Rubinoff *Collingwood and the Reform of Metaphysics. A Study in the Philosophy of Mind* (Toronto: University of Toronto Press, 1970).

A. Ryan 'A Conservative intelligentsia?', *Listener*, 111 (23 February, 1984), 10-12, 20.

J.H.M. Salmon 'Theory in historical context', *History of European Ideas*, 4 (1983), 331-5.

J.B. Sanderson 'Definitionism in politics', *Durham University Journal*, 57 (1964-5), 101-19.

—— 'Professor Oakeshott on history as a mode of experience', *Australian Journal of Philosophy*, 44 (1966), 210-23.

—— Review of W.H. Greenleaf, *Oakeshott's Philosophical Politics*, in *Durham University Journal*, 59 (1966-7), 120-1.

—— Review of R. Singh, *Reason, Revolution and Political Theory*, in *Durham University Journal*, 60 (1967-8), 47-8.

—— 'The historian and the "masters" of political thought', *Political Studies*, 16 (1968), 43-54.

—— Review of *Politics and Experience*, ed. P. King and B.C. Parekh, in *Durham University Journal*, 62 (1969-70), 130-2.

R. Scruton *The Meaning of Conservatism* (Harmondsworth, Middlesex: Penguin, 1980).

—— *A Dictionary of Political Thought* (London: Macmillan, 1982).

G.F. Seifert 'The philosophy of Hobbes: text and context and the problem of sedimentation', *Personalist*, 60 (1979), 177-85.

R. Singh 'On Oakeshott's traditionalism in politics', *Enquiry* (Delhi), 1: ii + iii (1964), 2: i (1965).

—— *Reason, Revolution and Political Theory. Notes on Oakeshott's 'Rationalism in Politics'* (New Delhi: People's Publishing House, 1967).

J.E. Smith Correspondence, *Cambridge Journal*, 1 (1947-8), 698-9.

J. Sobran 'Oakeshott looked ahead with his ideas', *Gazette Telegraph* (Colorado Springs), (27 December, 1990).

D. Spitz 'A Rationalist *malgré lui*: the perplexities of being Michael Oakeshott', *Political Theory*, 4 (1976), 335-52.

T.A. Spragens, Jr. *The Politics of Motion: the World of Thomas Hobbes* (Kentucky: University Press of Kentucky, 1973).

J.B. Stewart 'Hobbes among the critics', *Political Science Quarterly*, 83 (1959), 547-65.

K. Streitfthau 'Ammerkungen zur politischen Theorie Michael Oakeshotts', in M. Oakeshott *Rationalismus der Politik* (Neuwied und Berlin: Luchterhard, 1966), pp. 341-53.

A. Sullivan 'Taken unseriously', *New Republic*, 204 (6 May, 1991), 42.

M.P. Thompson 'Michael Oakeshott: notes on "political thought" and "political theory" in the history of political thought 1966-1969', *Politisches Denken*, 1 (1992), 247-50.

T.L. Thorson Review of *Politics and Experience*, ed. P. King and B.C. Parekh, in *American Political Science Review*, 63 (1969), 934-5.

E.W.F. Tomlin 'The philosophy of R.G. Collingwood', *Ratio*, 1 (1957-8), 116-35.

R. Tuck *Hobbes* (Oxford: Oxford University Press, 1989).

V.P. Varma 'Michael Oakeshott as a political philosopher', *Indian Journal of Political Science*, 36 (1975), 241-58.

J. Waldron 'Politics without purpose?', *Times Literary Supplement*, (6-12 July, 1990), 715-6 (review of P. Franco, *The Political Philosophy of Michael Oakeshott*).

W.H. Walsh ' "Meaning" in history', in *Theories of History*, ed. P.L. Gardiner (Glencoe, Illinois: The Free Press, 1959), pp. 296-307.

—— *An Introduction to the Philosophy of History* (London: Hutchinson, 1967; 3rd ed.).

—— 'The practical and the historical past', in *Politics and Experience*, ed. P. King and B.C. Parekh (Cambridge: Cambridge University Press, 1968), pp. 5-18.

P. Warner *Phantom* (London: Kimber, 1982).

H. Warrender *The Political Philosophy of Thomas Hobbes: his Theory of Obligation* (Oxford: Clarendon, 1957).

A. Watkins 'The Peterhouse connection', *Observer*, (27 November, 1977), 40.

—— *Brief Lives* (London: Hamish Hamilton, 1982).

J.W.N. Watkins 'Political tradition and political theory: an examination of Professor Oakeshott's political theory', *Philosophical Quarterly*, 2 (1952), 323-37.

C.C.J. Webb *The Historical Element in Religion* (London: George Allen and Unwin, 1935).

—— 'Religion, philosophy, and history', in *Philosophy and History*, ed. R. Klibansky and H.J. Paton (Oxford: Oxford University Press, 1936), pp. 53-60.

C. Welch 'Mrs. Thatcher's team: 4, Sir Ian Gilmour', *Daily Telegraph*, (7 July, 1978).

D. Wells 'Radicalism, conservatism and environmentalism', *Politics*, 13 (1978), 299-306.

D.M. White 'The right decision in politics', *Politics*, 13 (1978), 273-85.

D. Willetts *Modern Conservatism* (Harmondsworth: Penguin Books, 1992).

H. Williams *Concepts of Ideology* (New York: St. Martin's Press, 1988).

K. Williams 'A conservative perspective: a critical assessment of Michael Oakeshott's concept of education', *Irish Educational Studies*, 3 (1983), 33-46.

—— 'Science and the voice of Michael Oakeshott', *Rostrum: a Journal of Education and the Arts*, (1987), 121-8.

—— 'The voice of religion in the conversation of mankind', *Doctrine and Life*, 38 (1988), 395-404.

—— 'Learning to be virtuous and learning to converse: the treatment of

the theme of moral education in the writings of Michael Oakeshott', *Oideas*, 34 (1989), 94-104.
—— 'The dilemma of Michael Oakeshott: Oakeshott's treatment of equality of opportunity in education and his political philosophy', *Journal of Philosophy of Education*, 23 (1989), 223-40.
—— 'The gift of an interval: Michael Oakeshott's idea of a university education', *British Journal of Educational Studies*, 37 (1989), 384-97.
—— 'The classical idiom in curriculum design: a critical review of Michael Oakeshott's philosophy of the curriculum', *Curriculum*, 11 (1990), 132-9.
—— 'Authority and obligation in civil life: the limits of the formalist theory of Michael Oakeshott', *Studies* (Dublin), 80 (1991), 278-89.
M. Williams 'Liberalism and two conceptions of the state', in *Liberalism Reconsidered*, ed. D. MacLean and C. Mills (Totowa: Rowman & Allenheld, 1983), pp. 117-29.
P. Winch *The Idea of a Social Science and its Relation to Philosophy* (London: Routledge and Kegan Paul, 1958).
S. Wolin 'The politics of self-disclosure', *Political Theory*, 4 (1976), 321-34.
R. Wollheim 'Old ideas and new men', *Encounter*, 7 (October 1956), 3-12.
N. Wood 'A Guide to the Classics: the skepticism of Professor Oakeshott', *Journal of Politics*, 21 (1959), 647-62.
P. Worsthorne 'Notebook', *Spectator*, 244 (11 March, 1978), 5.
—— Correspondence, *Times*, (4 March, 1983), 11.
—— 'Diary', *Spectator*, 253 (1 September, 1984), 6.
—— Review of N. Annan, *Our Age*, in *Sunday Telegraph*, (7 October 1990).
—— Obituary, *Daily Telegraph*, (21 December, 1990), 19.
E. Young Correspondence, *Times*, (23 December, 1990), 11.

III. Unpublished Dissertations on Oakeshott

F.J. Abbate *Politics and Principles: a Critique of Michael Oakeshott's Conception of Rational Conduct* (Columbia University, Ph. D. thesis, 1970).
B.K. Barnett *On the Relation of Politics and Philosophy in the Thought of Michael Oakeshott* (Rutgers: the State University of New Jersey: New Brunswick, Ph. D. thesis, 1986).
D. Boucher *Revisionist Methods for Studying the History of Ideas: a Critical Analysis* (University of Liverpool, Ph. D. thesis, 1983).
W.J. Coats, Jr. *Michael Oakeshott and the Character of Experience* (University of Colorado, Ph. D. thesis, 1978).
S. Coleman *Reason in Tradition: the Political Philosophy of Michael Oakeshott* (Columbia University, Ph. D. thesis, 1966).

Bibliography

A.P. Ferretto *Oakeshott's Later Theory of Experience* (University of Manchester, M.A. thesis, 1979).

J.S. Fisher *Political Education: the Views of Michael Oakeshott and Paulo Freire* (Claremont Graduate School, Ph. D. thesis, 1980).

P.N. Franco *The Political Philosophy of Michael Oakeshott* (University of Chicago, Ph. D. thesis, 1987).

G. Graham *On the Nature of Ideological Argument* (Durham University, Ph. D. thesis, 1975).

T. Hall *Civil Association and the Common Good in the Philosophy of Michael Oakeshott* (Catholic University of America, Washington D.C., Ph. D. thesis, 1990).

I. Holliday *The Critique of Rationalism in Politics: Edmund Burke and Michael Oakeshott* (Oxford University, M. Phil. thesis, 1984).

—— *Individuality, Rationality, Civility. Michael Oakeshott's Writings on Politics* (Oxford University, D. Phil. thesis, 1989).

J.H. Liddington *The Philosophy of Michael Oakeshott and its Relation to Politics* (Oxford University, D. Phil. thesis, 1986).

T. Modood *R.G. Collingwood, M.J. Oakeshott and the Idea of a Philosophical Culture* (University College, Swansea, Ph. D. thesis, 1984).

N.K. O'Sullivan *The Problem of Political Obligation in the Writings of T.H. Green, B. Bosanquet and M. Oakeshott* (London University, Ph. D. thesis, 1969).

C. Phillips *John Stuart Mill and Michael Oakeshott: a case study of some differences in social policy and philosophical theory* (City University, New York, Ph. D. thesis, 1976).

A. Sullivan *Intimations Pursued: the Voice of Practice in the Conversation of Michael Oakeshott* (Harvard University, Ph. D. thesis, 1990).

K. Williams *Education and the Philosophy of Michael Oakeshott* (National University of Ireland, Ph. D. thesis, 1987).

Index

Abelard, 66
Annan, Noel, 82, 85
Aquinas, St Thomas, 65
Aristotle, 8, 55-6, 60f., 72
   Physics, 93
Attlee, Clement, 52, 84
Auspitz, Josiah Lee, 47 n.6
Ayer, A.J., 90

Bacon, Francis, 37, 51, 70
Barker, Ernest, 41
Bentham, Jeremy, 68
Berdyaev, Nicolai, 71, 101
Bodin, Jean, 103
Bolshevism, 48
Bosanquet, B., 103
Bradley, F.H., 10, 44
Brooke, Zachary, 89
Buckley, William F., 83
Burke, Edmund, 1, 58, 82, 84-5, 101
Burnham, James, 83
Butler, R.A., 84

Caligula, 95
Casey, John, 37
Cather, Willa, 3, 23, 71
Cellini, Benvenuto, 66
Cervantes, Miguel de, 84, 101f.
Charvet, John, 88
civil association, 12, 19ff., 55f., 77ff., 83, 102, 106
civilisation, 7ff., 40, 46, 71f., 73
Cranston, Maurice, 88
Collingwood, R.G., 11, 22, 44
   The Idea of History, 27

Communism, 14
Conrad, Joseph, 71, 81, 98
conservatism, 1, 54, 58f., 68, 75ff., 101, 104
conversation as metaphor, 7ff., 43ff., 47, 62f., 73
Cory, William, 50
Croce, Benedetto, 11

Dante, 85
democracy, 14, 19, 72
Dennison, S.R., 97
dialektikê, 8
Dilthey, Wilhelm, 7
Dinesen, Isak, 71
Dworkin, Ronald, 58

education, 7, 16-17, 43, 49ff., 62, 68, 80
Eliot, T.S., 59f., 84
Elton, G.R., 40
Emerson, Ralph Waldo, 69
enterprise association, 20, 77f.

Fabians, 4, 17, 67
Fascism, 14-15
Fisher, H.A.L., 94
Franco, Paul, 56, 77 n.10
Fuller, Timothy, 49 n.8

geistige Welt, 7
Gilbey, Alfred, 64
Gilby, Thomas, 64
Goethe, J.W. von, 100
Gonville and Caius College,

Cambridge, 4, 23, 64f., 67, 86, 104
Green, T.H., 103
Griffith, Guy, 63

Hayek, Friedrich A., 15, 102
Hegel, Georg Wilhelm Friedrich, 4, 8, 10-11, 13, 45, 55, 75, 94-5, 103
  Phänomenologie des Geistes, 4
  Philosophy of Right, 88
Heidegger, M., 102
Hempel, Carl, 93
history, 12, 22f., 32, 47ff., 88, 90ff., 104f.
Hitler, Adolf, 14, 52
Hobbes, Thomas, 31, 39, 50, 55, 65, 72, 103
  Leviathan, 4, 26, 38, 71, 97
Holt, J.C., 30
Hume, David, 27, 44, 68, 70, 84
Hunter College, 82-3

ignoratio elenchi, 4, 46

James II, King, 85
James, William, 82
Jewett, Sarah Orne, 23

Kant, Immanuel, 45, 96, 100
Keats, John, 62
Kedourie, Elie, 88

La Rochefoucauld, 37
Lane, Robert, 88
Laski, Harold, 16, 61, 67, 85, 104
law, rule of, 12f., 16, 19ff., 56, 79f.
Leavis, F.R., 58, 83
Letwin, Shirley, 56, 88
Letwin, William, 88
liberalism, 14
Locke, John, 13, 102
London School of Economics, 2, 16-17, 27, 32, 43, 59, 61, 67, 80, 85, 87, 97, 104f.
Louis XIV, 93
Lovejoy, A.O., 94
Lucas, J.R., 30

Mabbutt, J.D., 30
Macauley, Thomas Babington, 70, 99
Machiavelli, Niccolo, 26
Mackenzie, W.J.M., 35
Macpherson, C. Brough, 88
McTaggart, John Ellis, 12
Macmillan, Harold, 84
Maggioni, Guido, 37
Marx, Karl, 46, 50, 68
Mill, John Stuart, 1, 58, 70, 82, 103, 105
Minogue, Kenneth, 32, 34, 83
Mises, Ludwig von, 102
modality, 10ff., 14-15, 18ff., 25, 41, 45ff., 75, 82, 103f.
Montaigne, Michel de, 2, 37, 66, 68-9, 71, 84-5, 101f.
Mulino, Il (publisher), 38
Munz, Peter, 28

Namier, Lewis, 40
Nazism, 14-15
'negative capability', 62
Nozick, Robert, 58, 102
Nuffield College, Oxford, 59, 64

Oakeshott, Christel, 3, 23-5
Oakeshott, Michael, *passim*
  The Activity of being an Historian, 32, 49 n.7
  administrative skills, 17, 43, 98f.
  appearance, 3, 27f., 65
  The Civil Condition, 30
  The Concept of a Philosophical Jurisprudence, 12
  conversation, 5ff., 28f., 62, 66, 86-7, 89, 102, 105
  as editor and reviewer, 13f., 30, 33f., 97f.
  energy, 30
  Experience and its Modes, 4 n.1, 11ff., 18, 22, 27, 32, 39, 41, 43ff., 46 & n.3, 55, 76 n.8, 81, 84, 90, 103f.
  final illness, 25
  and friendship, 6, 25, 70, 98,

Index

102
generosity, 26, 30, 41
A Guide to the Classics, 63
Hobbes on Civil Association, 38-9, 81
hospitality, 23f.
Introduction to 'Leviathan', 26
learning, 4, 27, 33, 39ff.
and letters, 34f., 44
Leviathan: A Myth, 71 & n.2
modesty, 2-4, 28f., 33, 39, 44, 63, 65, 82, 102
On Being Conservative, 80 n.17, 81 n.18
On History and Other Essays, 12, 21ff., 31-3, 36, 39, 41, 81, 87-8, 93, 100, 104
On Human Conduct, 12, 18ff., 21-2, 32, 36, 38-9, 41, 45 n.2, 55ff., 65, 73 n.5, 74 n.6, 76 n.9, 77f., 78 n.12, 79 nn.13-15, 80 n.16, 81, 83, 91, 103
The Political Economy of Freedom, 77 n.11
Political Education, 26, 35f., 39, 52f., 67f., 74 n.7
A Place of Learning, 73 n.5
Rationalism in Politics, 8 n.6, 24, 26-7, 33, 35, 37-9, 43, 45 n.1, 46 n.4, 81, 83, 84 & n.1, 102
Rational Conduct, 26, 39, 41
religious beliefs, 14-15, 56, 65, 72ff., 85f., 92
romantic nature, 5, 49, 65, 70, 85
The Rule of Law, 21, 77 n.11
scepticism, 10, 71, 76, 84f., 103f.
sense of adventure, 10, 24, 59f., 65f., 70f., 102
The Social and Political Doctrines of Contemporary Europe, 14, 26
The Study of Politics in the University, 17 n.7, 30
teaching style, 5-6, 29f., 59, 80,
Chapter 7 *passim*, 99f., 105
The Tower of Babel, 21f., 39, 54 & n.11, 71, 72 n.3
The Voice of Liberal Learning, 6 n.3, 7 nn.4-5, 49 n.8, 81, 102
The Voice of Poetry in the Conversation of Mankind, 6 n.2, 12, 39, 46, 47 n.5, 51 n.9, 52 n.10, 70 n.1, 73 n.4
war service, 23, 43
writing style, 9, 34ff., 41, 43, 82f., 89f.
Ockham's razor, 20
Orr, Robert, 88
Ortega y Gasset, J., 101
O'Sullivan, Noel, 56
Oswald, Lee Harvey, 95

Pascal, Blaise, 37, 84, 101f.
Pater, Walter
 Marius the Epicurean, 4
 Gaston de la Tour, 71
Peirce, C.S., 23
philosophy, 9, 11f., 102, 104f.
Plato, 8, 45 n.2, 50-2, 71, 81, 84, 94, 104-5
Pocock, John, 28, 88
Polanyi, Michael, 75, 102
politics, 14ff., 17, 19, 51ff., 56f., 61, 75, 94f.
Popper, Karl, 93
Prior, A.N., 46
'Pursuit of Intimations, The', 53f.

Rationalism, 5, 12, 15f., 18, 51f., 57, 59f., 61f., 71, 75, 84f., 96, 104
Rawls, John, 58
Reader's Digest, 5
Rechtstaat, 21
Respublica Press, 23
Rimbaud, Arthur, 33
Rorty, Richard, 58
Rousseau, J.J., 94
Ryle, Gilbert, 37-8

St Augustine, 15, 65, 72, 75, 92

St Francis, 2
St George's School,
 Harpenden, 4, 80
St John of the Cross, 66
Sartre, J-P., 102
Searle, John, 49 & n.8, 50
Sévigné, Mme de, 34
Shakespeare, William, 71
Shelley, Percy Bysshe, 80
Shorthouse, J.H., 71
Sisson, C.H., 97-8
Skinner, Quentin, 31, 88
Socrates, 81
Spinoza, Benedict de, 10
Stebbing, Susan, 44
Stewart, Elinor Pruitt
 Memoirs of a Woman Homesteader, 5

Stokes, Eric, 94
Strauss, Leo, 4
Swift, Jonathan, 71

Thatcher, Margaret, 63, 68, 83
Thorp, I. Ernest, 88
tradition, 10, 12, 59ff., 76f., 85, 99
Trotsky, Leon, 15

University of London, 87

Vauvenargues, 37

Walpole, Horace, 34
Webb, Sidney and Beatrice, 67
Weisen, 11, 13
Wittgenstein, Ludwig, 38, 66, 96
Worsthorne, Peregrine, 63